Other Bestselling Books by Robert T. Kiyosaki & Sharon L. Lechter

Rich Dad Poor Dad

What The Rich Teach Their Kids About Money
That The Poor And Middle Class Do Not!

Rich Dad's CASHFLOW® Quadrant

Rich Dad's Guide to Financial Freedom

Rich Dad's Guide To Investing

What The Rich Invest In,
That The Poor And Middle Class Do Not

Rich Dad's Rich Kid Smart Kid

Give Your Child A Financial Head Start

Rich Dad's Retire Young Retire Rich

How To Get Rich Quickly And Stay Rich Forever

Rich Dad's Prophecy

Why The Biggest Stock Market Crash In History Is Still Coming . . .
And How You Can Prepare Yourself And Profit From It!

Rich Dad's Success Stories

Real Life Success Stories From Real Life People
Who Followed The Rich Dad Lessons

Rich Dad's Guide To Becoming Rich Without Cutting Up Your Credit Card

Turn "Bad Debt" Into "Good Debt"

Rich Dad's Who Took My Money?

Why Slow Investors Lose And Fast Money Wins!

Rich Dad Poor Dad for Teens

The Secrets About Money—
That You Don't Learn in School!

By Robert T. Kiyosaki
with Sharon L. Lechter, C.P.A.

WARNER BOOKS / LITTLE, BROWN AND COMPANY

New York ✃ Boston

Copyright © 2004 by Robert T. Kiyosaki and Sharon L. Lechter
All rights reserved.

Some material in this book is adapted from *Rich Dad Poor Dad: What The Rich Teach Their Kids About Money—That the Poor and Middle Class Do Not!* and *Rich Dad's Rich Kid Smart Kid: Give Your Child A Financial Head Start* by Robert T. Kiyosaki and Sharon L. Lechter. Adapted by Judy Gitenstein.

Published by Warner Books and Little, Brown and Company in association with CASHFLOW® Technologies, Inc.

CASHFLOW®, Rich Dad, Rich Dad's Advisors, Rich Dad's Seminars, the BI Triangle, and CASHFLOW® Quadrant are registered trademarks of CASHFLOW® Technologies, Inc. Rich Kid Smart Kid, Rich Dad Australia, Rich Dad's Coaching, and Journey to Financial Freedom are trademarks of CASHFLOW® Technologies, Inc.

 are registered trademarks of CASHFLOW® Technologies, Inc.

www.richdad.com

Warner Books • Little, Brown and Company
Time Warner Book Group
1271 Avenue of the Americas, New York, NY 10020

Visit our Web sites at www.twbookmark.com and www.lb-teens.com

First Edition

Library of Congress Cataloging-in-Publication Data

Kiyosaki, Robert T., 1947–
   Rich dad poor dad for teens : the secrets about money—that you don't learn in school! / by Robert T. Kiyosaki with Sharon L. Lechter. — 1st ed.
      p. cm.
   ISBN 0-446-69321-9
   1. Finance, Personal—Juvenile literature. 2. Entrepreneurship—Juvenile literature.
   3. Investments —Juvenile literature. 4. Wealth—Juvenile literature. I. Lechter, Sharon L.
   II. Title.
   HG179.K56495 2004
   332.024'00835—dc22   2004006069

10 9 8 7 6 5 4 3 2 1
Printed in the United States of America

Sneak Preview

Here's the book in a nutshell. Think of this as the trailer, the five-minute version of what you're about to read. . . .

Introduction: **Your Journey to Financial Freedom Begins Here**

You might be asking yourself, "Why should I be reading a book about money? I'm a teenager . . . I don't have much money." If that's the case, you're just the person I want to talk to. The sooner you begin to learn about money, the easier it'll be to get it—and the less you'll have to worry about it when you're older.

☞ **Part 1: THE LANGUAGE OF MONEY**

When it comes to money, "Think outside the bill!" You'll need a different mindset than the one you've probably grown up with in school and at home. This section talks about learning how to learn about money. And guess what? Anyone can do it!

Chapter 1: **Financial Intelligence: A New Way of Learning**

Did you know that if new information sometimes seems hard to absorb, the problem might be in the way you're being taught? How's that for a new concept? There's more than one way to learn. What's more, school may not be teaching you everything you need to know to make your way in life, especially when it comes to practical things like money. Read on. . . .

When I was growing up, my friend Mike's dad, whom I call my "Rich Dad," passed along his secrets of money to me. Now I will share them with you. . . .

Are your parents and teachers still telling you that getting a good education leads to a good job and financial security, a nice home, two cars in the garage, and lots of money for retirement? This may have been true when they were kids, but it's not true anymore. It's time to throw out that recipe and start with some new ingredients.

Everything you do, no matter how small or boring, offers learning opportunities. This chapter starts you thinking about the deeper meaning of cleaning your room, taking out the trash, or stacking cans on shelves.

Wouldn't it be great if we all could sit back and watch money roll in? If that were the case, you'd be reading a book about magic. It's possible, though, to have your money work for you without resorting to any magic at all, and this chapter will show you how I began to learn how to do it when I was just nine years old.

Life is filled with ups and downs, pluses and minuses, good days and bad. In the financial world we call these things assets and liabilities. One puts money into your pocket and one takes money out. This chapter shows you how to keep your pockets filled to overflowing and includes the ONLY rule you need to remember if you want to be rich. . . .

The rich stay rich because they know the secret of cash flow. They cover their expenses with income from their assets and flow the rest of their income back into assets. Seeing this explained in simple diagram form in this chapter will show how easy it is. No longer will you need to be intimidated by financial statements!

You heard it right: Playing games can be one of the most effective parts of the learning process. This is a fun chapter.

This section gives you some "nuts and bolts" information on money: how to make it, how to divide it up . . . and ways not just to hang on to it, but to make it grow.

Going to school might be your full-time job right now, but there is still plenty of time in the week to work on business opportunities AND get your homework done. In this chapter you'll learn the big difference between having a job in which you know exactly how much you're going to make each week, and creating interesting ways to make money, where you're the boss and the sky's the limit.

Here's an enticing thought: Pay YOURSELF first. Sounds good, doesn't it? This chapter outlines Rich Dad's philosophy of how best to divide up your money, along with the lowdown on what to do after you've filled your own piggy banks: Get that money moving! Actually, it's the best way to stay out of debt. But if you're already IN debt, turn to the next chapter. . . .

You must be wondering why a book about money would talk about NOT having money. Or, you're scanning ahead and ready to flip to this chapter first because you've made a bad judgment call and spent a little (or a LOT) more than you had. Unless you've just bought everyone in your family a high-performance sports car, chances are good that the damage can be corrected, but as you get older it gets much trickier. This chapter tells you how to climb out of debt before you get stuck too deep—and how to use a credit card the RIGHT way!

A few last thoughts before you head out into the REAL world—a world that offers opportunities at every turn to jump-start your personal success. There's no limit to what you can do if you believe in yourself. Ready, set, go!

Table of Contents

Your Journey to Financial Freedom Begins Here

✏️ Take This Quiz:

✔ Do you sometimes feel that what you're learning in school has nothing to do with your life?

yes / no

✔ Do you feel that school's not really preparing you for the real world?

yes / no

✔ When you want to buy something that's important to you, do your parents usually say they can't afford it?

yes / no

✔ Do you secretly worry that you won't be able to live the way you want when you're out on your own?

yes / no

✔ Do you really want to learn about money, but no one talks about it around your house or at school?

yes / no

If you answered "yes" to two or more of these questions, this book is for you. I struggled with these situations when I was growing up. I didn't always do well in school. I nearly had to repeat the tenth grade. Now I lead exactly the life I want—a life that includes complete financial freedom.

You may already be struggling to achieve financial freedom and independence in all parts of your life. Even though you might not have to pay rent or put gas in your family's car, there's a chance that you're already thinking about ways to afford your social life.

You may already be saving toward something big, like a new computer or a car. If that's the case, this book will help you make your money grow faster and you'll get what you want sooner. You may be struggling to figure out how to pay the high price of going to the movies once a week, or buying CDs, or buying a gift for someone special.

Whether you have an allowance or a job after school or on weekends, you may want to learn about budgeting and ways to stretch your dollar. If that's the case, this book is for you!

Or, maybe you're one of the many teens whose income is actually *necessary* because your parents aren't able to provide for the whole family. Many adults learned old-fashioned rules for financial security and then were surprised—and defeated—when the rules changed. Unfortunately, many of their children are also suffering as a result.

Rich Dad Poor Dad for Teens: The Secrets About Money—That You Don't Learn in School! covers some really important things I learned when I was growing up. My father taught me to get my education through schoolwork. My best friend Mike's father gave me a job and taught me about another type of education, one I learned in the real world.

I learned a lot from both dads. They each believed in education but had completely different views on money. One cared about money a lot (Mike's dad) and one didn't care very much about money at all (my dad). One worried about never having enough money (my dad). One thought about money and how to achieve power over it (Mike's dad).

My dad was highly educated, but even so, he used to say that he'd never be rich. He said, "Money doesn't matter." Mike's dad said, "Money is power." My dad always struggled to make ends meet. Mike's dad always had plenty of money. I needed them both to get where I am today. They taught me that there are many ways to be rich. Education is one way to be rich. Financial wealth is another way to be rich.

Rich Dad Poor Dad

In my career I've made enough money in business, real estate, and in paper assets to retire early and fully enjoy the great things life has to offer. I've also written a number of books. My first one, called *Rich Dad Poor Dad,* was about my own personal financial education. In the book I called my real dad "Poor Dad," and I called Mike's dad "Rich Dad." In labeling them this way, I wasn't criticizing either one of them. I was making a dramatic point about the different ways people think about money and the goals they set.

Rich Dad always told me, "If you want to do something—and you *think* you can—chances are, you'll get it done." Rich Dad always thought he could be rich—and he did get rich. *Rich Dad Poor Dad* was written to help people who really want to be rich to achieve their financial goals. The book caught on and became very popular. In the book, I offered some views about money that were different from what everyone was used to hearing, but that reflected the realities of today's changing economy—and the messages made sense to people of all kinds of backgrounds and experiences.

Now I travel and give speeches about *Rich Dad Poor Dad* and the other books I've written since then. People often come up to me with questions about how to teach their own kids about money, and so I wrote the book *Rich Kid Smart Kid* to help parents do just that. Now I've decided to write a book especially for teens—and you're holding it in your hands.

* * *

Financial Literacy

Congratulations for picking up this book! *Rich Dad Poor Dad for Teens* will teach you one of the most important subjects that isn't being taught in school: financial literacy. When people talk about literacy, they usually mean knowing how to read well. There's more to the story. Literacy is about being good at something. I would say it's about being able to speak the language of a certain field. Talking about money requires a whole new language. This book will help you become fluent in the language of money.

There are a lot of ways to be good at something. Being "good at" money doesn't always come easily. It's something you have to learn and practice. You may study economics in school, or even learn how to balance a checkbook in math class, but that's probably about the extent of financial education as part of the curriculum. And much of what's taught is "theoretical" instead of a real vocabulary for real-life situations. School is often about studying instead of *practicing*.

This book will pick up where school leaves off. It'll give you the language and understanding you need to feel confident about taking charge of your financial life, whether that means starting your own business or just being able to hold your own in a conversation with someone who might become your financial mentor—your own "Rich Dad." While some of your friends might be logging major couch time in front of the TV, getting nowhere, you may very well find yourself updating your financial statement, following your stocks online, or brainstorming about business ideas with other friends who, like you, want to own assets instead of liabilities.

Are you nodding your head "yes"? Or are you saying "*huh*?" to the terms I just mentioned? No matter how much or how little you know this minute, by the time you finish this book, you'll be able to speak the language of money more fluently. You'll begin to understand how money works and how it can work for you. Your journey to financial literacy starts right here, right now.

I actually started to learn about money when I was just nine years old, when Mike's dad—my Rich Dad—became my mentor. Now I'll share what Rich Dad taught me.

Thinking in Numbers

There are other books that tell you in detail how to open a bank account, balance a checkbook, and check a stock price. But they don't tell you how to *think* about money. Adults often view money as a "necessary evil"—something needed to pay bills, to count and recount, to obsess and worry about. There just never seems to be enough of it. But like it or not, money is something that will always be in your life, so you need to be comfortable with it—not afraid of it, like so many adults are. If you're educated about how money works, you gain power over it and can begin building *wealth.*

Financial literacy allows you to not fear money matters, and to see the real value of money. True wealth goes way beyond and is measured by more than cash. Success in life is more than financial success. This is what I learned when I was growing up, and it's my mission to teach this message to as many young people as I can so that the next generations will be responsible and knowledgeable—and powerful—when it comes to money.

School Is Just the Beginning

Unless you're planning to become a doctor or lawyer or go into a profession that requires a special degree, you may not need to go to any formal training programs after high school or college to earn money if you look for great learning opportunities in a job. In fact, you can be paid to learn in the real world instead of paying high tuition fees to learn in a classroom setting. Your financial education will train you on the job.

Am I saying that education isn't important? Not at all. Education is the foundation of success. I'm saying that school is just one place to learn. We go to school to learn scholastic skills and professional skills. For the most part, we learn financial skills out in the world.

Remember when you were first learning to ride a bike? Chances are, you started with training wheels and then one day you were ready for a two-wheeler. Perhaps someone held the bike for you until you felt steady—and then let go. You might have wobbled a few times or even fallen off once or twice. But most likely you got back on the bike and tried until you finally learned to balance, through trial and error and brain power.

Wouldn't it be funny if your parents had taken you to a special bike-riding school? It would have been a waste of their money. There are things you learn in school and things you learn in life—like how to walk, tie your shoes, ride a bike, and most things that have to do with money.

A new *type* of education is what I'm talking about. The best doctor in the world might have a great medical education but not know anything when it comes to finances. He or she might save a life on the operating table but have trouble running an office that makes money.

Amazing, isn't it, to think that you might be getting knowledge that your doctor—or your parents—might not have? Now that's power!

Journal: What Do I Want?

You know about journals. Sometimes you have to keep them in school for English class. But the best journals are the ones that you keep for yourself—where you let your deepest thoughts about your real life just spill out. Putting your feelings on paper feels good—and sometimes it helps you express something that was bothering you that you didn't even know was buried deep inside.

Writing about your feelings about and experiences with money is one way to help figure out where you are and where you want to go financially. A journal can create a place where you don't have to feel guilty or strange about talking about money. Remember, part of my goal is to help you feel comfortable and powerful with a subject that's often taboo at home or in school. You can start making something that seems abstract feel *real* by putting your thoughts on paper.

Get yourself a notebook—green (for money) would be a good color!—and different colored pens to keep nearby as you read this book. Your "Rich Dad Journal" can help you plan your own financial journey as you learn more about mine.

Why not start by writing down all the things that you want? Let your brain buzz with ideas, as if you were creating a birthday wish list. Write in different colored pens—it helps you be more creative—and draw pictures if you like. Doodling is a good thing! The list you create doesn't have to be just money-related. (Sure, you can write down "car," but you can also write down "make cheerleading squad" or "get lead in school play.") Carry your notebook with you during the day to jot down ideas or thoughts that come to you. What do you want in your life?

Writing in your journal will also help you chart your progress while reading this book. Keep in mind that you're writing for yourself, with no grades and no one judging you. Your journal is a very safe place.

Part 1

The Language of Money

Chapter 1

Financial Intelligence:
A New Way of Learning

You Are Smart

First of all, let's get one thing straight: You are smart! I wanted to make sure you know that from the very beginning. When I was growing up, my dad always told me that everyone is born smart—that every child has a special kind of genius. I loved that idea. Even though I didn't always do well in school, I kind of knew the reason didn't have to do with me. I wasn't stupid. I just learned in a different way than the way teachers in school expected me to.

My father taught me to have a good attitude about learning. He taught me to find my best way of learning. If I hadn't done that, I might have flunked out of high school or college. I probably wouldn't have been prepared for my financial life. And I wouldn't have had the confidence to be who I am today.

We all learn differently. The trick is to find the way you learn best. When you do that, you'll discover your own personal genius.

A genius is someone who excels at something. But a genius isn't necessarily good at everything. In fact, a genius usually has a special ability in one area while being pretty average in others.

Did you know that Albert Einstein, who thought up the theory of relativity ($E = mc^2$), never did well in school? He wasn't good at memorizing things, yet he grew up to become one of the greatest mathematical thinkers of all time. His brain focused on ideas rather than facts. Facts, he said, could be found in books, so he never felt the need to keep facts in his head. He wanted his head clear to think creatively.

School asks us to keep facts in our head, but when we're out of school, we usually just need to know where the facts are kept so we can look them up or know whom to call when we need them!

The way our performance is measured in school has very little to do with how intelligent we really are or how successful we can be. The way we perform in school is usually just a measure of how well we take tests! It's not a true measure of the genius you were born with.

* * *

✎ Everyone Is Born a Genius

Take out your notebook again and write a list of people you know. Try to get to twenty names. Include people from school, family members, even teachers. Put your name at the top of the list. Next to each name write down what that person is good at, no matter what it is. Do you have a friend who can't sit still and is always tapping his foot to some beat that's inside his head? Write that down. Can your sister do the crossword puzzle in ten minutes using a pen without even once glancing at the dictionary? Write that down, too. Can you fix almost any computer problem? Put it in the book.

This exercise helps you do a couple of things. It's the first time in your financial journey where you'll be asked to try to see something that you didn't see before—to look at something in a new way. Seeing talents in others you hadn't really recognized leads you to see your own talents. Knowing what your strengths are is one step toward success. Knowing how to detect other people's strengths is also a great skill, since creating a solid, reliable team is critical if you plan to build a business or be an investor someday.

The Myth of IQ and Intelligence

I remember that every once in a while in school, we'd have days when we were given all sorts of tests. The tests were described as "standardized." I was always puzzled by that idea. Every person is unique, so why were we all being evaluated in a cookie-cutter kind of way? The truth is that no two people are alike.

Later I found out that the tests were measuring our IQ, which stands for "intelligence quotient." An IQ number is supposed to represent a person's ability to learn facts, skills, and ideas. But a person's IQ really boils down to this: It's a number that shows the relationship between a person's "mental age" (as measured on a standardized test) and his or her chronological (real) age. Then this number is multiplied by 100 and the result is your IQ. When I was growing up, people thought that an IQ stayed the same for a person's whole life. How limiting! Fortunately, that thinking is changing.

Over the years I've done a lot of reading and research about intelligence, especially about the way people learn. IQ can relate to academics, but it can also relate to other things, like sports. When I was young, I had a high baseball IQ. My friend Andy had a very high academic IQ. Andy had an easier time learning in school because he learned by reading. I learned by doing something first and reading about it later. One formula worked for Andy, and another one worked for me. We each developed our own winning formula.

Everyone Has a Special Learning Style

In those IQ tests in school, only one type of intelligence was being measured: a person's aptitude, or talent, for words. But what if someone's not a word person? I don't especially like to read, so does that mean that I am stuck with a low IQ? Today, the answer is no. In 1983, a psychologist named Howard Gardner published a book called *Frames of Mind* (Basic Books). In it, he describes seven different types of intelligence, not just one. He also argues that people's IQ can change.

Dr. Gardner's list of intelligences, which he also calls learning styles, has created a new road map for learning new skills and information, whether it's rocket science, threading a needle, or financial literacy.

What's *Your* Learning Style?

Take a look at this list. As you read it, think about what methods best describe your learning style. Circle the number that matches up for each of the learning styles: 1 is least like you and 5 is most like you.

This is not a test. I repeat: *This is not a test!* There's no good or bad answer or high or low score. This is just a way to think about how you learn most comfortably.

❖ **Verbal-linguistic intelligence** If you always have a book tucked in your backpack, circle 5. This type

of intelligence has to do with reading, writing, and
language. It's also called being "word smart."

1   2   3   4   5

✧ **Numerical intelligence** If you're one of those people
who can do a math problem in your head, circle 5.
This intelligence is found in people who easily
grasp data and numbers. They're also usually calm
and rational thinkers.

1   2   3   4   5

✧ **Spatial intelligence** If doodling helps you listen in
class, or if you're always seeing things that you'd
like to photograph, circle 5. This intelligence is used
to see patterns, designs, and space—and is found in
many artists, architects, and choreographers who
can visualize a two- or three-dimensional object or
event and make it real.

1   2   3   4   5

✧ **Musical intelligence** Are you tapping a pencil or
drumming your fingers right now? Head for the
number 5. This type of intelligence is especially
tuned in to sounds, rhythm, and rhymes.

1   2   3   4   5

✧ **Physical intelligence** If you love PE in school, or if
your room looks like a sporting-goods store, you're
physically intelligent—someone with awareness of
how to use your body well, like many athletes and
dancers.

1   2   3   4   5

✧ **Interpersonal intelligence** Do friendships seem effortless to you (mark 5) or endlessly complicated (mark 1)? Do you always (or never) know what your friends are thinking—or are you somewhere in between? Mark it down. This intelligence refers to the way someone gets along with other people, which is also called "being people smart."

   1 2 3 4 5

✧ **Intrapersonal intelligence** If interpersonal intelligence is "being people smart," intrapersonal intelligence is "being self-smart," or self-aware. It's also called emotional intelligence, because it relates to the way you handle your emotions, such as fear and anger. Do you understand your own reactions to difficult situations and can you control them? Do you think before you talk back? Are you patient with your own shortcomings and do you take care of your self-esteem?

   1 2 3 4 5

Recently Dr. Gardner has come up with an eighth intelligence:

✧ **Natural Intelligence** describes a person's sensitivity to the world around him or her. If you enjoy being outdoors every weekend or are involved in school or community groups working for the environment, circle 5.

   1 2 3 4 5

I've talked a lot with a psychologist who taught innovative learning at Arizona State University about various learning styles and how they help us achieve personal and financial success. Listening to her thoughts, I've added one more intelligence:

✧ **Vision** is what determines who will be a leader and who will be a follower. Great leaders can see how a situation will play out and take action in response. Winston Churchill, Prime Minister of England during World War II, was one of the world leaders who was against the Nazis from the start. It's as if he could see the terrible things that would happen if they stayed in power. Those of you with crystal balls, mark 5.

    1   2   3   4   5

Do you notice a pattern to your numbers? Where did you rank yourself highest?

If you ranked yourself a 4 or 5 in verbal-linguistic intelligence, it's likely that you are comfortable with reading and writing as tools for learning. If you ranked yourself a 4 or 5 in physical, musical, or natural intelligences, it's possible that you may have great success in "learning by doing"—using on-the-job training such as internships or being involved in school and community clubs. If you ranked yourself a 4 or 5 in spatial or numerical intelligences, you may benefit from learning through drawing, making charts and diagrams, building models, or working with your hands. If you ranked yourself a 4 or 5 in inter-personal or verbal-linguistic intelligences or vision, you may learn best by talking with friends or grown-ups about their experiences, by debating, or by performing. You'll find your intrapersonal intelligence useful in any type of training, since it will help you maintain your patience and self-esteem in the face of challenges.

It's also possible that you ranked yourself high in several areas. That means that you'll be comfortable with "mixing and matching" different activities that work with your learning styles.

But what if you didn't rank yourself high in *any* area? Are you doomed? Not at all. This exercise was designed to help you start to think about *how* you think. People who think about the future, who have "vision," for example, are likely to become good business leaders. But that doesn't necessarily mean they are *now.* If you don't feel you have vision now, don't panic. You can "pump up" any area if you're determined to exercise your brain, just like Rich Dad told me to do when I was a kid.

If you're stronger in one area than others, there's a lot you can do to balance out. Here are some suggestions. What other ideas can you come up with?

✧ **Talk about money** at home and with your friends to develop your verbal-linguistic and interpersonal intelligences.

✧ **Read about it!** Lots of magazines about money and finance show how money works in *real life*, rather than in textbook math problems. The more you learn now about how the experts manage and invest their money, the more inspired you'll be to manage your own. (Verbal-linguistic and numerical intelligences)

✧ **Write about it!** Use your Rich Dad Journal to explore ideas about the role money plays in your life now and in the future. (Intrapersonal and verbal-linguistic intelligences and vision)

✧ **If you get an allowance, take it seriously.** Think of it as part of your income. Make up an invoice for your parents. Figure out ways to earn it and invest it. Manage your own money rather than treating your allowance as a handout. (Numerical and interpersonal intelligences)

✧ **Do your own audit.** Once a week, do an accounting of where your money has gone. (Numerical intelligence)

✧ **Decide to become responsible for your future.** Create a positive attitude about money. Envision the future for yourself. (Intrapersonal intelligence and vision)

Finding Your Winning Formula

Unfortunately, the style of learning that is taught in school may not always be the style you are most comfortable with.

The ways in which we learn—which might be a combination of learning styles—add up to our winning formula.

Let me return to the example of my friend Andy and me. As I said, I loved to play baseball. I had a high physical intelligence. I also loved to learn about players' statistics. I had a pretty good numerical intelligence. After I had learned all I could about the game from playing it, and had learned all I could about the players from other kids (interpersonal intelligence), I then turned to books to get more information. This style, of trying things out first and then reading about them later, has become my winning formula—one that I use to this day.

My friend Andy's winning formula began with books. His strength was verbal-linguistic. He loved to read about and study things before he tried them out. He might have made a good manager for a baseball team while I would have made a good player. We were very different and we each figured out what worked best for us.

Developing Your Financial IQ

Are you beginning to see that any fears or stumbling blocks you may have about money may have to do with how you learn? If verbal-linguistics is not your thing, then, like me, you'll learn by doing and seeing. Later in this book I'll talk more about learning by doing, and you'll see some concepts explained through pictures and diagrams. Reading this book will also help you develop your intrapersonal intelligence by exploring your goals and fears—and by building your self-esteem.

👆 Rich Dad Q&A

What do learning styles and winning formulas have to do with getting rich?

I'll bet a lot of people who are voted "Most Likely to Succeed" every year in your school yearbook are the people with the best grades. While some of those people will eventually become successful, some of them may not. And it may very well be because they never learned financial intelligence. Many of them will be surpassed in wealth by people like you who are determined to find financial freedom. Discovering your learning style and your personal genius is the first step to having confidence—confidence that allows you to see and pursue opportunities, and to take risks.

The road to a high financial IQ is to work on your money skills using the intelligences that work for you—and work to develop the others so that your whole brain is working full-steam. Try a few different learning styles on for size. It might not be until the second or third try that you feel you're working with the right combination.

Take out your Rich Dad Journal and make a list of all the activities you do after school and the subjects you do well in. Chances are you'll see a connection between what you do well in and what you enjoy doing. You may also find that there are one or two intelligences from the list that your activities relate to. These are your strengths. The next step will be to find a way to leverage your strengths into financial success by finding financial opportunity.

💡 Put Your Brain in Motion

Say this sentence: "I can't afford the things I want."

Now say: "How can I afford the things I want?"

One statement stops you from thinking. The other revs your brain and gets you thinking. If you said the first sentence to me, I'd think you'd made up your mind that you won't *ever* get what you want. But if instead you asked, "How can I afford the things I want?" I would think you were serious about finding solutions. I would view you as positive and forceful.

When Rich Dad was my mentor, he would say, "My brain gets stronger every day because I use it. The stronger it gets, the more money I make." This book will put your brain in gear.

Believe It

Tomorrow, listen to yourself as you talk to people throughout the day. How do you sound to others? Determined? Tentative? Do you believe what you are saying—or do you sound like you don't believe in yourself?

The best way to get what you want is to believe you can get it. Thoughts are powerful. You can make things happen if you set your mind to it.

Here's something you can do to track your belief in yourself: Write down on a piece of paper or index card one statement that describes how you feel about money. It could be something like, "I'll never be rich." Use the piece of paper or index card as your bookmark and check in on your feelings about this statement as you read this book. In the middle of the book, you might write on it, "I will be rich." By the end of the book you might very well cross off the other two sentences and write, "I *am* rich."

All right, you may not really be rich *yet*. The point I'm making is that turning a thought around can create a mindset that will make something happen. That intention teamed with the financial education you'll get from this book is a powerful combination.

Next up: Rich Dad's secrets about money.

Part 2

Rich Dad's Money Secrets

Chapter 2

Rich Dad's Money Secret: The New Rules for Making Money

The Old Rules Don't Apply Anymore

One of the most important things I learned when I was a kid was that when you play a game, you've got to know the rules, because rules define how to succeed at the game. But sometimes, in the real world, rules can change— and that can turn your world upside down if you're not prepared.

Here's a "rule" that you've probably heard: If you study hard and do well in school, you can go to a good college, learn a profession, graduate, get a good job, make lots of money, and be a success in life.

What if I told you that having a profession is not the only way to earn money—especially if you want to make a *lot* of money? Having a job will certainly earn you a living, but working for a salary isn't the most effective path. This path will probably lead you right into the Rat

Race—where you work to earn, work harder to earn more, and eventually burn out.

In order to explain this better, I'm going to tell you a little bit about my years growing up.

The Rich Think Differently

My dad was superintendent of education for the state of Hawaii. Though my father was well respected, he didn't make lots of money—or at least, not as much other kids' fathers, who drove nice cars and owned beach houses.

Because of where my family lived, I went to the same public school as the rich kids. If I'd lived on the other side of the street, I would have been assigned to a different school district and gone to school with kids from families more like mine.

By being in school with kids who were rich, I could see that they had a different outlook about money. My dad was always worried about making ends meet and worried about the future. Parents of my friends seemed so confident about the future. They actually *thought* differently about money, I realized.

I also knew that the rich kids learned things at home that I wasn't learning in my house. They learned to have a confident attitude about money. Some of them even talked about money at the dinner table. In my family, money was talked about in whispers, if it was talked about at all. Money was a taboo subject.

From my earliest childhood, I decided I wanted to be rich. I decided I liked the idea of having money and all the nice things it could buy. I liked the idea of enjoying life instead of working all the time. I also liked the idea that rich parents wouldn't have to worry about paying bills and supporting their kids as much as my dad did.

A Magic Formula for Getting Rich?

When I was nine years old, I asked my dad how to get rich. He told me, "If you want to be rich, you have to learn to make money." I'm sure he had no idea how closely I would follow his advice. The results were pretty comical—but they led me to my first big discovery about money.

In school, my best friend Mike and I spent lots of time together, and we hung out after school, too. We were partners in everything. In a way, we even shared each other's dad!

Mike's dad worked at the sugar plantation in town. He didn't have much of an education (in fact, he never went past the eighth grade), but he was always looking for business opportunities.

My dad and Mike's dad were very different. I would sum up their difference this way: My dad said, "The love of money is the root of all evil." Mike's dad said, "The lack of money is the root of all evil."

A Moneymaking Scheme

Like me, Mike wanted to make some money, just like my dad suggested. So we became business partners. Here's what we did . . .

After collecting toothpaste tubes from everyone in the neighborhood, we melted down the tubes, which in those days were made of lead. Then, very carefully, we poured molten (really, really hot!) lead through a small hole in the top of milk cartons from school. We had created plaster of Paris molds in these milk cartons.

What were we doing? We were making lead nickels. We were literally *making money*! We had no idea that all U.S. currency was minted by the federal government and that what we were doing was illegal.

While we were working, my dad came home with a friend. When I innocently explained that we were just *making money*, like my dad had suggested, they got a really good laugh. After they stopped chuckling (and after we found out what "counterfeiting" was), my dad couldn't help but be impressed. "You boys have shown great creativity and original thought," he said. "Keep going. I'm really proud of you!"

Think Rich, Be Rich

Great . . . but my dad's advice wasn't helping us in our quest to be rich. I decided to come right out and ask him, "So, how come *you're* not rich, Dad?"

"Because I chose to be a schoolteacher," he told me. "Schoolteachers really don't think about being rich. We just like to teach." Then he said, "If you boys want to learn how to be rich, don't ask me. Talk to Mike's dad."

"*My* dad?" Mike asked in surprise. Mike's dad wasn't rich at the time. "But we don't have a nice car and house like the rich kids at school," Mike told my father.

"That's true," my dad said. "You don't have those things now. But your father and I both go to the same banker, who says your father is brilliant when it comes to making money. Your father is building an empire and I suspect that in a few years he will be a very rich man."

Excellent! Mike and I had no idea about his father's magic touch with money. We got really excited. After we cleaned up the mess that our counterfeiting scheme made, we headed over to Mike's house. When his dad heard the story, his reaction was, "You're on your way to thinking like the rich think." That's what we wanted to hear. Now we were psyched. Of course, we had no idea *what* it was we were thinking that made us "think rich."

* * *

💡 What You Think Is What You Get

My two dads' very different views on money taught me that "what you think is what you get!"

WHAT MY POOR DAD SAID	WHAT MY RICH DAD SAID
Poor Dad: "Study hard so you can find a good company to work for."	**Rich Dad:** "Study hard so you can find a good company to buy."
Poor Dad: "The reason I'm not rich is because I have you kids."	**Rich Dad:** "The reason I must be rich is because I have you kids."
Poor Dad: "When it comes to money, don't take risks."	**Rich Dad:** "Learn to manage risks."
Poor Dad: "Work for benefits."	**Rich Dad:** "Be totally self-reliant financially."
Poor Dad: "Save."	**Rich Dad:** "Invest."
Poor Dad: "Write a good resume to find a good job."	**Rich Dad:** "Write a strong business and financial plan to create a good company."

The Haves and the Have-Nots

People sometimes talk about the "haves" and the "have-nots," and that the "haves"—the rich—think differently. The rich often own the companies for which others work. The rich own stock in the companies while others get paychecks. This fact leads to a different frame of mind, to say the least.

If you work in a job with a specific salary, then chances are you're not going to have much vision beyond your paycheck. Sometimes I see people in restaurants or on trains doing simple multiplication on napkins or scraps of paper. They're multiplying an amount of money by the number "52."

They're calculating their annual income—what they make each year. No matter how many times they do the calculation, the number stays the same. But let's say you're thinking like a rich person. Your work is to discover ways to make extra money without working longer hours, ways to start your own business. Your work is to discover new possibilities. Sounds exciting, right?

What I learned from my first moneymaking venture was that it was possible to "think rich," and that it was possible to make a *choice* to be a "have" or a "have-not." My dad seemed comfortable with his decision to be a "have-not," but I knew that I wasn't. I was beginning to see that being rich had something to do with creating opportunities, not just accepting that you lived on one side of the street or another.

I couldn't wait for my next moneymaking adventure— or, at least, my first *legal* moneymaking opportunity. And one presented itself very soon afterward.

✎ Quiz: Are You a Team Player?

Mike was my first business partner, and together we came up with our business plans. You, too, can go into business with someone. But are you a team player? Circle "Yes" or "No" after each statement below based on your *real* feelings about them—not how you think they "should" be answered.

1. Two heads are better than one.

       Yes   No

2. Working with someone can be more fun.

       Yes   No

3. Working on my own can be very lonely.

       Yes   No

4. I need my own cheering section when work is slow.

       Yes   No

5. I might make more money working as part of a team.

       Yes   No

6. I like to do things my way. Better not to compromise.

       Yes   No

7. I don't want to share the profits.

  Yes   No

8. I like to be my own boss.

  Yes   No

9. I can work faster and more efficiently on my own.

  Yes   No

Give yourself 1 point for each "no" and 2 points for each "yes" in questions 1 through 5. Give yourself 1 point for each "yes" and 2 points for each "no" in questions 6 through 9.

If you scored 15–18, then you might be considered a team player. If you scored 12–14, you're on the right track. If you scored less than 12, you might think about ways to strengthen your interpersonal skills. Why? Because one of the best ways to become financially free is to become a successful business owner—most of whom surround themselves with strong team members.

Working with someone can be very rewarding, emotionally and financially. It allows you to bounce ideas off another person. You may not be sure where to begin or what direction to take on your own. With someone else, it's easy for one idea to lead to another and—presto!—money is created.

☞ Rich Dad Q&A

Why isn't this book called *Rich Mom Poor Mom?*

It could be. I just happened to grow up being influenced by my dad and my best friend's dad. Rich Dad was my mentor and a father figure. Your mentors can be your mom, a friend's mom, or a female teacher. Knowledge about money is by no means the domain of men. Some of the most powerful people in business today are women.

If you want to find out more, pick up a copy of *Fortune Magazine.* Every year since 1998, this money magazine has been publishing a list of "The 50 Most Powerful Women in Business." Take a look at the current list and you will find women listed from all fields from film companies to banks to eBay. Women who make it on that list get there not just for the money they earn but also for their influences on the media and mass culture. Oprah Winfrey is the perfect example of someone who fits all those categories. On the international scene, J. K. Rowling (author of the Harry Potter books) now has more money than the Queen of England!

Chapter 3

Rich Dad's Money Secret: Work to Learn, Not to Earn

A Different Kind of Learning

Let's face it: You might be looking at the title of this chapter thinking that "working" and "learning" aren't high on your to-do list. Or maybe you're thinking, "*I have to work to earn. My family doesn't have much money.*" Whether or not your family needs the income, having a job is also a way to learn and identify opportunities to start your own business. As you might have already guessed, this book is about a *different* kind of working, and a different type of learning.

My First Job

After Mike and I "made" our first batch of money, my dad told us, "You're only poor if you give up. The most important thing is that you did something. Most people only talk and dream of getting rich. You've done something. I'm very proud of the two of you. I will say it again. Keep going. Don't quit."

We didn't quit. We talked to Mike's dad, just like my own dad had suggested. Mike's dad worked for the sugar plantation, but he also owned warehouses, a construction company, a chain of stores (superettes), and three restaurants. He offered us a job at one of the superettes for ten cents an hour.

"You work for me," he said, "and I'll teach you, but I won't do it classroom-style. I can teach you faster if you work, and I'm wasting my time if you just want to sit and listen, like you do in school. That's my offer. Take it or leave it."

Mike's dad was talking about a whole new kind of learning. We took the job. Even though I had questions, even though I had ball games I wanted to play in, I felt (using my "intrapersonal intelligence" and my "vision," qualities I didn't know I had at the time) that this was the right thing to do.

And so my on-the-job, hands-on financial education began. Mike and I reported to Mrs. Martin, who ran one of the stores that Mike's dad owned. She put us to work dusting and re-stacking canned goods in her store. To tell you the truth, it was one of the most boring things I've ever done. This was *working*? I'm not quite sure I had much of an idea of what working was all about, but I sure didn't think it was this: taking down cans, dusting them, and putting them back. It was steaming hot in the store, too. Every weekend I thought angrily about all the things I expected we'd learn that Rich Dad had promised. When was *that* going to start?

Mike and I hated every minute of our job. After three weeks of working on the weekends, I was completely fed up and ready to quit. I felt angry, cheated, and exploited. We were doing all this work for just ten cents an hour! Even in 1956, that wasn't much money at all. I decided I had to do something about it. I was going to talk to Mike's dad.

Standing Up to My Boss

The next Saturday, I went to Mike's house at eight o'clock in the morning. "Take a seat and wait in line," Mike's dad told me, and disappeared into his little office next to a bedroom. So I waited in the living room with other people who worked for Mike's dad who also wanted to have a meeting with him . . . and waited . . . and waited.

Eventually, I was the only person left, and still Rich Dad didn't come out of his office to call me in to speak with him. I could hear him inside, talking on the phone and rustling papers. That made me furious. I could imagine steam coming out of my ears, like in a cartoon. Rich Dad was wasting my whole Saturday morning! I was sitting in his dark, musty living room on a beautiful, sunny Hawaiian day.

When Rich Dad finally signaled for me to come in, I was angrier than I had ever felt in my life. I told him everything that was on my mind. "You promised to teach me and you aren't holding up your end of the bargain," I accused. I was standing up to a grown-up and it felt good, but scary at the same time.

Instead of being angry with me, Rich Dad seemed pleased that I'd spoken up. "So," he asked, "Does *teaching* to you mean talking, or a lecture?"

"Yes," I answered.

"That's how they teach you in school," he said with a smile. "But that's not how life teaches you, and I would say that life is the best teacher of all. Most of the time, life does not talk to you. It just sort of pushes you around. Each push is life saying, 'Wake up and learn.'"

That made me think about what I was learning. Ever since I had started working, all I thought about was money, money, money. I thought about how little I was making and how little I would get for each hard day's work. I didn't want money to have such control over me. I wanted to "be the money's boss" instead.

Rich Dad said that when life pushed me around, I needed to push back. By going to Rich Dad to tell him my problems with the job, I had learned to push back. But rather than be angry at Rich Dad, I needed to take action.

✍ Rich Dad Q&A

Is "pushing back" always the right thing to do?

Not always. Even though Rich Dad taught me to "push back," he also taught me not to let my emotions—especially fear—make my decisions for me. Here are some examples of things you might say when emotions are doing the thinking and making the choices.

What You're Saying: My grade is low because the teacher doesn't like me. I might as well not even bother studying for the next test.	**What You're Thinking:** People are against me.
	What You Fear: I'm destined to fail.
What You're Saying: My friend is always talking to me in class, so I can't do my best work.	**What You're Thinking:** It's his fault, not mine.
	What You Fear: I don't have control over this situation.
What You're Saying: I don't have a trust fund like my rich friend. I don't see the point in trying to become rich if I have nothing to start with, like she does.	**What You're Thinking:** I resent my friend because she has financial security and I don't.
	What You Fear: The odds are against me.

When a situation "pushes your buttons," take a step back and try to assess the situation coolly, using your inter- and intrapersonal intelligences. These skills will also help you in the business world when working with difficult people.

💡 What Did Your First Job Teach You?

Even if you're pretty young, you may have already started working—regardless of whether or not you're getting paid. Do you do chores around the house? Are there things you regularly take care of, like shoveling snow off the driveway, raking leaves, or taking out the trash? Then you've already had your first job. You may not get paid to do chores around the house, but you should learn about sticking to what you've started by fulfilling your responsibility.

Do you know people who leave a trail of unfinished projects? Maybe even you're one of those people who's made a habit of starting a project and stopping when you don't feel like working on it anymore. It's okay to start something and then decide it's not right for you, but being financially successful means learning to follow through with your plans. Besides, finishing a job—and doing it well—is a great feeling.

What It Means to Work

So I did some real thinking about working and about money.

I had made a commitment. I was working for a specific amount of time. I couldn't just stop when I felt like it, even if I was tired. I had a responsibility to honor.

And, I was doing something for Mrs. Martin that she needed to have done, and she was paying me. At first, that seemed like a pretty fair exchange, but I didn't feel that the money that I was earning was worth the ball games I was giving up to do the work.

Rich Dad told me, "Money is an illusion." He told me to imagine a donkey dragging a cart with its owner dangling a carrot in front, moving the carrot further forward with every step the donkey takes. The donkey will never reach that carrot, yet it keeps trying. The donkey is chasing an illusion.

This is true with working, Rich Dad explained. The carrot is like a toy. The toys we want get bigger and bigger and more expensive as we get older. When we're young, we may be happy to drag around the same old raggedy stuffed animal. By the time we are teenagers, we want more and more. This is natural! The advertising industry doesn't want us to be content with what we have. Ads on TV and radio, in movies, and almost everywhere we look on the street, in malls, and on highways show us hip and beautiful people with the latest cell phones, computers,

CDs, and clothing. As we're bombarded with these images, it's virtually impossible to resist the urge to think that "more," "bigger," "more expensive," or "newer" equals "better."

Adults fall prey to these temptations, too. Adults have toys as well. Theirs are even bigger and more expensive, and include cars, boats, motorcycles, big-screen TVs, furniture, landscaping, and second homes. The stakes get higher when buying these toys.

So what's the solution? People who are already rich seem to know it: Work to learn and to have your money work for you. Rich Dad wanted me to find the power to create money rather than to work for money. He taught me not to *need* money. "If you do not need money," Rich Dad said, "you will make a lot of money." This sounded like a major contradiction, but when I thought about it sitting in his office that day, it began to make sense.

Rich Dad taught me some important lessons about gaining power over money and power over myself. I learned not to blame Mrs. Martin, my boss, or other people for my own desires and for my own decisions. I learned to take responsibility. I learned not to let money bully me.

✎ **Create Your Own "Think Tank"**

When you do repetitive tasks as part of a job or chore, it may seem like counting sheep at bedtime—boring enough to put you to sleep! But the truth is that if you have the right attitude, doing a repetitive task can be meditative and energizing. It actually provides an opportunity for quiet time that can free your mind to do some creative thinking . . . and creative thinking is key in Rich Dad's secrets for success!

Chapter 4

Rich Dad's Money Secret: "My Money Works for Me"

Life Is Filled with Surprises

I may have been just a kid, but I'd survived a tough business meeting with Rich Dad. I had stood up to him and he had seemed to be saying it was okay. Amazing! Rich Dad patted me on the back and suggested I get back to work. The next thing he said to me caught me by surprise. "This time, I will pay you nothing."

"What?" I was floored. If working for a salary wasn't going to make me rich, how could working for *no* money do anything other than make me stupid?

But that's when it really hit me. I was supposed to "*work to learn, not to earn.*" At this point, I had started to see that I really could trust Rich Dad. Somehow, I had to believe that dusting and stacking cans would teach me *something*, because I wasn't going to get a single penny for my time.

So, Mike and I continued to work for no salary. At one point, Rich Dad offered us as much as $5.00 per hour, but by then, we were on to him. "Nope," we said. He was testing us. He was dangling a carrot in front of our noses. He was trying to tempt us with something that would give us instant gratification, but we'd learned in our "Rich Dad after-school enrichment program" to wait for something much bigger.

I was right. Rich Dad said, "Keep working, boys, but the sooner you forget about needing a paycheck, the easier your life will be when you are adults. Keep using your brain, work for free, and soon your mind will show you ways of making money far beyond what I could ever pay you. You will see things that other people never see. Opportunities are right in front of their noses. Most people never see these opportunities because they're looking for money and security, so that's all they get. The moment you see one opportunity, you will start seeing opportunities for the rest of your life."

Seeing what other people never see. . . . That sounded good. Very soon after that, Mike and I had the chance to see something that others had missed. We were able to create our first real business opportunity.

A Comic Twist

One day, a few weeks later, I noticed Mrs. Martin cutting the front page of a comic book in half and throwing the rest of it into a large brown cardboard box. I asked her what she was doing, and she told me that she was going to get credit for the unsold comic books. The distributor needed to see only the part of the front page she was returning. The rest of the comic book was no good to her or to the distributor. But it could be a gold mine for Mike and me.

We talked to the distributor the next time he came into the store. "You can have these comics if you work for this store and do not resell them," he told us. A light bulb went on in my head. Mike and I were soon in business again, and this time it was with a real moneymaking plan.

A Surefire Business Opportunity

Here's how we figured it: A comic cost ten cents each in those days. Most kids could read five or six comics in one sitting. That would come to sixty cents if they bought the comics. But if they came to a place where they could just read the comics without buying them, and if we charged them an admission fee, they would come out ahead—and so would we.

I cleaned out the spare room in the basement and in it we opened our comic-book library and reading room. We charged ten cents admission to any kid who wanted to come and read comics during two hours each weekday that our library was open.

A lot of kids used our library. We averaged $9.50 per week over a three-month period. Do the math! We were on our way to being rich.

We kept our job at Mrs. Martin's store, and that allowed us to get the comics. We even collected unsold comics from the other superettes in the chain. We kept our promise to the distributor and we kept our commitment to Mrs. Martin and Rich Dad.

The best part about our comic-book business was that we were making money even when we weren't there. We'd hired Mike's sister to be our librarian, and she ran things for us. The operation was smooth—all she had to do, really, was keep everything neat and take the money from each person who came in. The business practically ran itself. Our money was working for us!

✎ Is There a Business Opportunity Staring YOU in the Face?

Mike and I stumbled on our comic-book business— which means it was right there in front of us. Is there an opportunity in front of you that you can't see yet?

Go back and review the wish list of things that you want that you created in the beginning of the book, or make one now. Now go back to pages 17–20 to look at the list of intelligences and learning styles to remind yourself of your strengths. Okay, now think about ways to put these things together.

Here's the kind of thing I have in mind: Let's say that one thing you've been wanting is a great costume for a friend's huge Halloween party. You noted on pages 17–20 that you're spatially intelligent—you happen to be good at doing things with your hands. Why not get your friends together and show them how to make costumes? You can come up with the costume ideas and drum up business by printing flyers on your computer to drop off with all the neighbors (as well as all of the people going to the party), offering them your team's service for a fee. You can pay your friends with the money you earn and still make money yourself. As long as the costumes get done, everyone makes money— and you don't even have to do all of the work.

Keep your eyes and ears open. The next time you hear the words "I wish we had . . . ," think about whether there's a way you can create a business to meet that need. Don't assume that grown-ups are the only ones who can do it. Plenty of community needs can be met by the efforts of teenagers. Just remember, whatever service you're providing, work toward building a bigger business where money can be made even when you *aren't* working.

Chapter 5

Rich Dad's Money Secret:
Create Money

Where Does Income Come From?

Where does money come from? It sounds like a dumb question, but you'd be surprised by how many people don't know the complete answer to it. Often, when we're growing up, we don't get the chance to think about money in concrete ways. When we're born, all of our needs are taken care of. As if by magic, food appears on the table and we have clothing, heat, water, and electricity. The phone works when we pick it up. As a child, we don't always connect the dots between our parents leaving for work in the morning and their coming home at night with all the clothing, supplies, and food the family needs.

As we grow up, we realize that all of these things don't appear by magic. They are paid for with money.

Somehow, money enters the picture, but we don't always see all of the ways that this happens. It's *not* all in the paycheck.

Types of Income

There are actually three ways to earn money. Going out and working at a job is one of the ways. It's the most direct and the most visible way, so it's the one that people think of first. But there are two other ways to make money that are actually more effective.

The three basic types of income are:

✧ **Earned income**. Earned income is money you get from working. When you have a job, you're paid a salary—usually in a paycheck you get every week or every two weeks. When my Poor Dad told me to "get a good job," he meant to work for an earned income.

✧ **Passive income**. Passive income is earned even when you're not physically doing any work. The money Mike and I made from our comic-book business was passive income. Money made from real estate is passive income. This is how I made my money for many years, and it was an extremely good way. I bought apartment buildings, and then leased the apartments to people who paid me every month to live there.

Passive income can also come from businesses that you set up that someone else runs on a day-to-day basis. The comic book business that Mike and I set up worked this way.

Passive income could also come from royalties— income that comes in from writing a book or a song or from appearing in a commercial that is on TV or the radio. Every time a book is sold, a song is sung, or a commercial is aired, the people who were involved usually get some money. Sometimes the money is just a few pennies, but those pennies can add up to become a lot of dollars.

People who are rich are usually good at generating passive income. Their money is working for them while they're working in other ways—managing their portfolio, starting other businesses, or simply enjoying their lives.

❖ **Portfolio income**. If you have money invested in paper assets (stocks, bonds, or mutual funds), you have portfolio income. Portfolio income works on the same principle as passive income. Your money is working for you even when you're asleep!

* * *

📢 Rich Dad Q&A

What's the best kind of income?

Rich Dad often told me, "The key to becoming rich will be your ability to convert earned income into passive income and portfolio income." He also told me that the taxes are highest on earned income and lowest on passive income. When he told us this, it was clear that the best kind of income was the kind that worked hardest for us and cost us the least: passive or portfolio income.

Knowing the best kind of income to generate is probably the *second* most important thing we needed to remember. The *most* important thing that Rich Dad told us we needed to remember was . . . (Drum roll, please!)

The Only Thing You Need to Remember Is . . .

One day, when Mike and I were in Rich Dad's office, he told us that if we wanted to be rich, there was really only one thing we needed to remember: "Know the difference between assets and liabilities," he said, "and buy assets."

When Rich Dad told us this, we thought he was kidding. We had been working with him for a while, waiting for the secret to getting rich, and this seemed a bit anticlimactic—even dull! "Rich people acquire assets," he continued. "The poor and middle class acquire liabilities, but they *think* they are assets."

"You mean all we need to know is what an asset is, acquire them, and we'll be rich?" I asked.

Rich Dad nodded. "It's that simple."

"If it's that simple, how come everyone isn't rich?" I asked.

Rich Dad smiled. "Because people do not know the difference between an asset and a liability."

It took Rich Dad only a few minutes to explain the difference between assets and liabilities.

Assets = Money in Your Pocket

Rich Dad's first definition, which I've never forgotten, was that an asset puts money into your pocket. An asset should generate income on a regular basis.

The traditional definition of an asset is anything that you own that is worth something—that could be "turned into money" if you needed it to be. Look around your room. Is there anything that might be worth something? You probably have more than you think . . . a computer, a TV, a cell phone? Skis? An excellent baseball glove? A collectible Barbie Doll? A collection of Beanie Babies from when you were younger, or Nintendo?

Your assets also technically include the balance in any bank accounts in your name, or the current value of stocks or bonds that you bought or that were given to you. And, of course, the cash you have in your wallet. The cash could be from your allowance, from a job, or a gift someone gave you.

But here's the catch: While you might consider everything of value in your room an "asset" (because you could sell it for decent money on eBay), it's not really an asset until it is sold. Why? Because it's not putting any money into your pocket until then. (And then, it's no longer an asset because it no longer belongs to you!) Same thing goes for the cash in your wallet: sitting in your wallet, your cash is not secretly reproducing itself, putting more money into your pocket. That would be a dream come true, wouldn't it?

In a way, it's not just a dream. There are places *other* than your wallet where cash "reproduces itself"—when it's invested in assets that give you passive and portfolio income. Anything that you own that produces passive or portfolio income is an asset.

Liabilities = Money out of Your Pocket

Liabilities are the opposite of assets. Liabilities take money out of your pocket. In fact, a lot of the things mentioned above—the TV or computer in your room that might traditionally be considered "assets"—are actually liabilities right now, because it took money *out* of your pocket to get them. And many of them, when converted to cash, would give you back less money than what you paid to buy them.

Liabilities also include everything that you owe. If you borrow money from a friend, or from your sister or brother, the debt is a liability. If your parents took out a mortgage on your home and have to make payments, that's a liability, too. If you pay for something with a credit card, creating debt, that's a liability as well. And, of course, the taxes you need to pay are a liability.

Asset or Liability?

Poor Dad: "Our home is our largest investment and our greatest asset."

Rich Dad: "My house is a liability, and if your house is your largest investment, you're in trouble."

Hmm . . . So a house can be an asset AND a liability? Yes, actually. Assets can be deceiving. Something that might seem like an asset can turn into a liability. Here's an example: A couple gets married. They decide to live in the apartment that one of them lived in before they were married. After all, two can live as cheaply as one, they figure. But the apartment is tiny. They decide to save money to buy their dream house one day. After that, they'll start a family.

The couple has two incomes and they spend a few years working hard and focusing on their careers. Their incomes go up . . . and so do their taxes. In fact, the more they earn, the more taxes they must pay. Their expenses go up too, but that's their own doing. Each time one of them gets a raise, they go out and celebrate. They get a bigger TV. They trade in their car for a nicer model. They save a little money.

Finally, they do buy their house. They are proud of their first asset. Soon, though, they discover they have to pay a property tax, a very high one. And their new house is much bigger than their apartment and they have many more rooms. Next they buy furniture.

Since they were renting their apartment and couldn't take the appliances with them when they moved, they buy a stove, a refrigerator, a washer and dryer. Most of the rooms need air-conditioning. They buy four units and their electric bill goes up during the summer months. Every month they make a mortgage payment to the bank to pay off the loan they took out to buy the house.

Their beautiful house, their so-called asset, has become a liability. The reason? It's taking money out of their pockets—and it's not putting any money into their pockets. It's that simple. This is the way Rich Dad explained it to Mike and me, and it's never been confusing since.

You might be saying, "Well, this can't happen to me, because I don't own a home." But don't be so sure. Suppose you buy a car. The car seems like an asset, but paying for gas takes money out of your pocket each week. Then, one day it breaks down and you must pay to get it towed to the service station. Parts are expensive. In no time, your asset has turned into a liability. In addition to guzzling gas, your car is guzzling money. On top of that, the resale value begins to go down from the day you purchased it. Maybe you could sell it for parts and get enough money for a couple of lunches at school. . . .

Let's say your parents buy a house. The house is in good condition when you buy it, and it's on a quiet, tree-lined street. Soon a big shopping center opens near you and suddenly the house is in a great location. Because of its desirable location, the house goes up in value. If your parents were to sell it they would probably get a lot more for it than what they paid. But . . .

Let's say that soon after, a twenty-plex movie theater opens in the shopping center and suddenly your quiet street is bumper-to-bumper with honking horns and angry drivers and the air is filled with exhaust fumes. Your house value takes a nosedive. Until the traffic is rerouted (or until stronger laws against horn honking are enacted), your quiet country lane is noisier than Times Square on New Year's Eve.

To make it worse, one cold winter's day, the water heater breaks down and the roof starts to leak. All of a sudden, your parents start pouring money into a house they thought was a safe purchase. Not any more!

Let's go back to your room. Your computer, and all the

other technology on and around your desk, was state-of-the-art, top-of-the-line, and up-to-the-minute when you bought it. The minute you got home, though—in fact, the second you opened the cartons—your equipment began to depreciate (or go down) in value.

Think about the latest cell phone you just had to have because it beeped a certain way or had a camera built into it. Well, now there are phones that make better music or take even sharper pictures. Soon, there will be a new model on the market (say, the 6.0 model instead of the 5.0 model—the higher number always makes you *have* to have it). Suddenly the cell phone in your backpack now won't be worth the plastic it's made of.

I call these things "doodads." Doodads go down in value the minute you buy them.

When Rich Dad explained all of this to Mike and me, we just stood there silently, waiting for him to tell us what to do. The solution, I'm happy to say, is an easy one that most people know about but often don't act on: Buy assets that produce income. And that's how I made my fortune. The apartment buildings I own and rent out apartment by apartment may cost me money to run, but they're a steady source of income, too.

What's a *teenager* to do, you might be asking? Buy carefully. Don't overspend on doodads. Look at your assets! Have you collected things that have grown in value? Look through your room again and take good care of those CDs, autographed letters, photos, or baseballs, as well as your Beanie Babies. Someday they may sell for more than you paid for them—but there's no guarantee.

Better yet, keep your eyes and ears open for ways you and your friends can start a business. A business might eventually turn into something that produces passive income. And once you have money from your business, try to buy stocks and bonds that will grow in value and be income-producing assets.

So . . .
✔ Assets put money in your pocket.
✔ Liabilities take money out of your pocket.
✔ Buy assets that produce income.

All clear? Let's move on.

Chapter 6

Rich Dad's Money Secret:
It's All About Cash Flow

Financial Statements: Reading the Numbers

"If you want to be rich, you've got to read and understand numbers," Rich Dad told Mike and me hundreds of times. To keep things simple, Rich Dad taught us by using as many pictures—and as few words—as possible. The first thing he drew was a diagram to show us the easy way to keep track of assets and liabilities: the financial statement.

The financial statement shows the relationship between what you have and what you owe. It's something that accountants and people running businesses (both large and small) rely on to do their jobs and keep their businesses running smoothly. A financial statement is a snapshot of what your monetary situation looks like at any given moment. It's made up of two parts: an income statement and a balance sheet.

An income statement is also called a profit and loss statement, which actually describes its purpose more clearly. It simply shows what money is coming in and what money is going out and gives you an idea at a glance of what money you might have available. It represents income and expenses over a specific period of time.

A balance sheet shows the relationship (and sometimes the tug-of-war) between assets and liabilities. It is a snapshot of one moment in time.

The pattern of money coming in and going out is called cash flow.

Rich Dad showed us a few very simple drawings. If you want to reproduce these for your own financial statement, take a clean sheet of paper and draw a series of four boxes in a pattern that looks like this:

Income
Expense

Assets	Liabilities

The top half of the financial statement, the income and expense boxes, is your income statement. The bottom portion, the asset and liability boxes, is your balance sheet.

A financial statement tells us where our money is. And ideally, we want more income than expenses, and more assets than liabilities. By looking at the cash flow pattern, we can see which direction our money is going.

The Cash Flow Pattern of an Asset

This is what the cash flow pattern of an asset looks like.

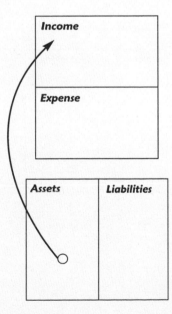

The arrow, representing the flow of money, is going from the assets box to the income box, meaning that the asset is generating money.

This is the cash flow pattern of someone who is rich.

The Cash Flow Pattern of a Liability

The cash flow pattern of a liability would look like this:

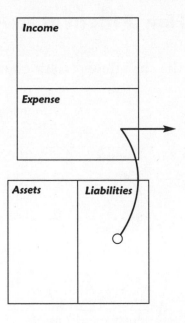

The cash flow arrow would go from the liabilities section to the expense section, and then it would go off the chart, meaning that the money is gone. All the money has been used to take care of what you own.

✎ Rich Dad Q&A

Is it possible to have money and still be poor?

Yes. This seems like a contradiction, but it can happen. The amount of earned income is not directly proportional to your total wealth. My dad had "a good job" that paid a decent salary, but he never broke his Poor Dad habits. Mike's dad might have earned almost the same (or even less) money than my dad from his job at the sugar plantation, but he invested it well and became rich.

Poor Dad's financial statement would look like this:

On the other hand, Rich Dad's financial statement would reflect fewer expenses in relation to the amount of his income. His liability box would be much smaller than his asset box. His financial statement would look like this:

```
┌─────────────────────────┐
│ Income                  │
│                         │
│                         │
├─────────────────────────┤
│ Expense                 │
│                         │
│                         │
│                         │
└─────────────────────────┘
┌───────────┬─────────────┐
│ Asset     │ Liability   │
│           └─────────────┘
│           │
│           │
│           │
└───────────┘
```

So, as you can see, if you keep as much in the asset box as you can and as little in the liability box as you can, you'll be rich. It's that simple.

Create Your Own Financial Statement

Now it's your turn! Using the same four boxes (labeled *Income, Expense, Asset, Liability*), you can easily create your own financial statement.

Let's start with income. Do you have a job after school or on weekends? This will be the number one item on your income sheet. Add anything else that represents money coming in: your allowance, plus any cash gifts.

Now let's turn to the money going out. What are your expenses? Make a list of absolutely everything you can think of that you spend your money on. Create categories, too. Here are some examples to get you going. As you read through this list, circle all the items that you buy on a regular basis and note how much money, on average, you spend in each category per month.

- ◇ **Food:** sodas, candy, popcorn at the movies, meals out, snacks
- ◇ **Clothing:** footwear, school clothing, weekend clothing, accessories (purses, belts, jewelry)
- ◇ **Sports items:** clothing (uniforms, bathing suits), footwear (hiking boots, sneakers for specific sports, Rollerblades), equipment (surfboard, skateboard, bike, tennis racquet)
- ◇ **Transportation:** Public (bus, subway), private (taxis, cars), gas, tolls, cost of tune-ups or repairs
- ◇ **Entertainment:** movies (tickets, rentals), CDs,

DVDs (purchase or rentals), magazine subscriptions, books, concert tickets, cell phone bill

❖ **Drugstore items:** shampoo, nail polish, deodorant, makeup

❖ **Beauty and grooming:** haircuts, manicures/pedicures

❖ **Pet supplies:** food, kitty litter, collar, leash, toys

❖ **Big-ticket items:** airline tickets, new car, school tuition, contributions toward family expenses, cell phone

How many items did you circle? There's a good chance you circled items in all of these categories. You may even have more items to add. As you can see, your money probably won't have a chance to sit around on your income sheet for too long.

Your parents' expense statements will include many more items, such as rent or mortgage payments, maintenance, utilities (gas and electricity), car upkeep (gas and repairs), education for their children (you!), vacations for themselves and the family, taking care of their own parents who are getting older, and parties.

When you think about it, it's amazing that there is ever any money left in the income section. Expenses can be . . . expensive!

Did you notice that most of your spending seemed to fall in a few different categories? Or are you not quite sure where your money goes? There's an easy solution to this: Save the receipts.

Every time you take out your wallet to pay for something, ask for a receipt—yes, every time, even if you just buy gum. This gets you to think about your purchase. Being aware of how your money is spent will make you think twice before you buy something. Instead of "I *have* to have that," you might also start to think, "Do I have something similar at home?" Pretty soon you'll see that each dollar will go a lot farther because it will stay in your wallet a lot longer.

✎ Where Does Your Money Go?

Do you leave your house with money in your wallet and come home with almost nothing—even though you've only been out for a couple of hours? Either there are some very good pickpockets in your area or you're spending your money without even realizing it.

Here's an exercise: Keep track of what you spend in your Rich Dad Journal for just one day. If you can find a tiny notebook, put it inside your wallet so that you'll see it when you need to pay for something. You could also put a rubber band around your wallet and your notebook to keep the two things together. Every time you buy something, write it down.

Using this rubber band/notebook method will make it harder to get to your money. It will increase your awareness of how often you reach for your wallet.

Don't forget to carry a pen or pencil with you.

Where Are You Financially?

So, you've done your income statement by filling in your income and expenses. Now it's time to work on the balance sheet. If you have any stocks, bonds, or bank accounts of any kind, write them down in your asset box. You'll also need to fill in their value in dollar amounts. It's easy to know exactly how much you have in a bank account, but you may need to estimate the value of your stocks and bonds.

Next, list the value of any liabilities you might have: a car loan or any debt you might owe to others—anything that takes money out of your pocket every month.

To get your net worth, subtract the liabilities from the assets. Your net worth should be a "plus," or positive, number. If you have more liabilities than assets, your net worth will be negative. If you owe more than you have, then you'll need to review your financial plan. And it's definitely time to think about your budget.

Mind Your Own Business

When we truly know the difference between an asset and a liability, we'll be able to start buying real assets. And you'll be able to keep your asset column strong. Once a dollar goes into your asset column, think of it this way: That dollar becomes your employee. This is a really great example of making money work for you. By "minding your own business," you will truly be on your way to financial independence.

✎ Stretching the Dollar

If you know what you spend your money on, you'll be able to make decisions about how to trim your spending. Try it for a day and you'll see how often you buy things without thinking. Try it for a week and you may find yourself coming home with about the same amount of money as you left with. In addition, there are lots and lots of ways to stretch your dollar. Here are some examples.

✔ Think about ways to "recycle" old clothing. Don't like that T-shirt you bought at the height of your pink phase? Dye it.

✔ Instead of having lunch out all the time with your friends, have lunch at someone's house. With all the great cooking shows on TV, simple meal ideas are easy to find. This is a guaranteed way to have fun and keep costs down at the same time.

✔ If there are any supplies that you buy on a regular basis—shampoo, paper, or batteries, for example— buy them in bulk and buy them on sale. You'll always save money this way and you'll have a supply ready at home when you need it.

Chapter 7

Rich Dad's Money Secret: Play Games to Learn

Poor Dad: "Study to learn."
Rich Dad: "Play games to learn."

Play to Learn!

Rich Dad never did anything the way we expected. That's what kept Mike and me on our toes and kept us loving what we were learning. Rich Dad had explained the huge concepts of assets and liabilities with simple drawings. Next, he had something else amazing in store for us.

Rich Dad used to say, "Games are a reflection of real life. The more you play, the richer you become." What a great concept—life represented by a game board. I loved it! I had always loved playing Monopoly®. Now my teacher and mentor was telling me that playing Monopoly would teach me about money.

The game Monopoly is all about real estate on the surface, but it uses all of the principles about money, such as assets and passive income, that I introduced in the last chapter. When you play Monopoly, every time you go around the game board, you collect $200. From what I was learning from Rich Dad, I realized this was like getting a salary—or earned income—and if I managed to hang on to the money and put it somewhere that would earn money, I'd have an asset.

Even as a young boy playing games like Monopoly, I was interested in real estate. I would buy houses or a hotel every chance I had during the game. That meant that every time another player landed on a square where I owned property, they would pay me rent. My assets were earning income, which translated into money with which I could buy more assets. I had learned that from Rich Dad, but now I was seeing it in action. The sky was the limit in terms of the money I could bring in.

I began to get the idea of how this would translate to real life—and real cash flow. If I owned a building or apartment house and people rented apartments in that building, money would come in on a monthly basis.

Because I loved Monopoly so much as a kid, I developed my own game as an adult that taught some of the things that Rich Dad taught me. I now have three board games: *CASHFLOW® 101* and *CASHFLOW® 202*, for adults, and *CASHFLOW® for KIDS*. The games are also available as e-games. They are *CASHFLOW® THE E-*

GAME (101) and *CASHFLOW® for KIDS at Home.* There's even a special version for teachers to be used in the classroom: *CASHFLOW® for KIDS at School.*

If you own *CASHFLOW® THE E-GAME (101)*, you can join our subscription Web site, Rich Dad's *INSIDERS*, and play the game online with people around the world. Go to www.richdad.com to find out more. All the games allow you to put the concepts and goals you're learning in this book to the test, and it's just as fun (if not more) than a game of Monopoly, because it reflects the real world you live in today.

From the Rat Race to the Fast Track

The idea of all of my games is to get out of the Rat Race— that endless cycle of earning money and paying bills—and move to the Fast Track, where your assets are earning money for you and you're getting passive income.

In Chapter 2, I talked about new rules. The old rules I described—going to school, getting a job, buying a house, making a salary—led people to a life in the Rat Race. In the Rat Race, all you do is work, pay bills, work harder, make more money, buy more doodads, pay higher bills, work even harder, and continue to pay bills rather than spend more time enjoying life and having the freedom to give to others. Ninety percent of the population lives in the Rat Race, always struggling to pay bills and living from paycheck to paycheck. They think that getting a raise is a solution to their problems, but getting more money usually means wanting and buying more liabilities—something we learned from the couple you read about in Chapter 5. Buying more liabilities leads people even deeper into the Rat Race, and deeper into debt.

Rich Kid Smart Kid

We also developed a Web site for kids with four mini-games (at www.RichKidSmartKid.com) that teaches about profit, debt, money management, assets, and the importance of giving back through charity. You can select games from different age categories (kindergarten through high school) for a great review of all the concepts from this book.

One of the games is called "Jesse's Ice Cream Stand." The goal is to help Jesse make a profit from his ice cream business so he can take a vacation. He needs to figure out which flavors to sell and what prices to charge in order to make the most profit based on demand and carton price. In another game, you can help Jesse finally get out of the Rat Race and onto the Fast Track by building assets—that is, helping him figure out how to expand his ice cream business all over town. Different types of assets work better in different locations around his town. By analyzing his return on investment for each, you can begin to clearly see how money can work for you even when you're not working. More on "return on investment" in Chapter 10—or, go straight to the Web site right now (www.richkidsmartkid.com) to check it out.

In "Reno's Debt," you get to help Reno play a game called "Cheese Run" at the amusement park—but he needs to get some money in order to play the game. In this game you learn about borrowing bad debt (where you have to pay it back) and borrowing good debt (where your investment pays it back), working to get out of debt, and getting the best return on your investment.

The third game on the site, "Ima's Dream," is about giving money to charity. The best way to do this is to pay yourself first—that's using your money wisely. As she earns, Ima puts money into the three banks: for giving, saving, and investing. We'll learn more about these banks in Chapter 9.

CASHFLOW® FOR KIDS AT HOME

If you buy the CD-ROM version of *CASHFLOW® for KIDS at Home*, you'll see that there are three age-level choices: ages 5–7 (which you can play with a younger sister or brother), ages 8–10, and ages 11–14. Both the 8–10 and 11–14 versions of the game challenge you to get out of the Rat Race by finding ways to make money through passive income (and yes—we've learned about all these things already in this book!).

You can play the game alone or with other players. Each player begins the game with some money and some income. What you do from there is up to you! Each player rolls the dice (or rather, clicks on the virtual dice) to move around the board. You can land on a red, green, or yellow square, representing expenses, business opportunities, or a "sunshine" card, which means that you have the chance to do something good for others. When you land on a green square and are offered a business opportunity (like buying a building), you have to decide whether it's a good opportunity or a bad one, based on the facts you're given about the opportunity. You can try it—or you can decline the offer and save your money. You can even print out your balance statement to get a picture of your finances at any time during the game.

CASHFLOW® 101

In *CASHFLOW® 101*, just as in *CASHFLOW® for KIDS*, the goal is to get your income from investments (your passive income) to be greater than your expenses so that you can go out and pursue your dreams rather than worry about working for your paycheck. In this game you have the chance to pursue some of those dreams, such as having dinner with the president or building a kid's library or visiting the seven wonders of the world.

The game allows you to practice being a good investor at four levels of investing: the small deal, the big deal, the Fast Track, and *CASHFLOW® 202*. In the process of playing, the game teaches you about investing and accounting. As I say in the rules: "Financial literacy wins the game!"

📣 Rich Dad Q&A

Isn't playing games kid stuff?

Not at all. Playing games is like getting a vitamin-packed dose of real life in a safe and entertaining setting. When you play *CASHFLOW®*, for example, you're put into new financial situations with each roll of the dice or click of your mouse. This is instant experience without spending real money. With a board game or electronic version, we can get the benefit of years of experience in just a few hours of playing. The game allows you to see (in a very short amount of time) that you have financial options.

✎ What Kind of Player Are You?

I've watched *CASHFLOW*® being played by more than one thousand people, and I've gotten feedback from countless others. What kind of player are *you*? Do you see yourself in these descriptions? Rate each description on a scale of 1–5. Circle the number that best describes you: 1 would be least like you and 5 would be most like you.

1. **Gets out of Rat Race quickly.** Often the people who get out of the Rat Race the fastest are the people who understand numbers and who have creative financial minds. These people recognize their options quickly. People who take the longest are people who don't feel comfortable with numbers and who don't see the power of investing.

   1   2   3   4   5

2. **Sits on "nest egg" too long.** I've noticed that people who gain lots of money in the game often don't know what to do with it. They might have money but others in the game seem to be getting ahead of them. This is true in real life, too. There are a lot of people who have a lot of money but don't get ahead financially.

   1   2   3   4   5

3. **Believes "Nothing good ever happens to me."** I've noticed that some people playing the game

complain that they're not getting good opportunity cards. They're not landing on the "good" squares. So they just sit there while others play. I know people who do that in real life. They wait for the "perfect" opportunity, as opposed to taking risks.

1   2   3   4   5

4. **Says "I can't afford it."** I've watched people get a card that represents a good business opportunity but then say they don't have enough money to take advantage of it. These people tell me that they would've gotten out of the Rat Race if only they'd had more money. These people just sit there, too, while others play the game. They do this in real life, as well. They see all the great deals coming, but they say they have no money to cut the deals.

1   2   3   4   5

5. **"It's right in front of my nose, but I can't see it."** I've noticed people get the right card, read it out loud, and yet not realize it's a great opportunity. They have the money, the time is right, and they have the card, but they can't see the opportunity staring them in the face. They don't see how it fits into their financial plan for escaping the Rat Race. I know more people in this group than in all the others combined. Most people have an opportunity of a lifetime flash right in front of them, but they just can't see it.

1   2   3   4   5

Do you see yourself in any of the descriptions of different types of players? All of the people I've described here are adults. Often the people who get the game most easily are young people because they're willing to take risks. I'm guessing that because you're reading this book, you're most like the player in Example #1. If you aren't, don't worry! Play the game enough and you'll see your playing style change.

I notice that rich people who play the game don't ever sit on the sidelines. They participate, they're creative, and they take "calculated" risks, meaning that they think through their plan with great care, even though the plan might be considered risky by others.

Learn to Make—and Create—Choices

I hope you're getting the picture: Playing games like *CASHFLOW*® is really good practice for life. It's a way for you to make use of all your learning styles, to strengthen your financial intelligence, and to think rich. As your financial IQ gets higher and higher, you'll be able to avoid the Rat Race in real life.

Financial intelligence means creativity in solving financial problems. If opportunities aren't coming your way, what else can you do to improve your financial position?

How many options can you find? If an opportunity lands in your lap, and you have no money, and the bank won't give you a loan, what else can you do to get the opportunity to work in your favor? If what you've been counting on doesn't happen, how can you turn a lemon into lemonade—or in this case, millions?

Playing the Game of Life

I've spent years developing my financial intelligence because I want to participate in the fastest and biggest game in the world. I want to use my mind to the fullest. I want to be where the action is. It's "what's happening," it's what's hip—and the more I experience, the more exciting it becomes. At first it may seem like a roller-coaster ride from the Rat Race (where Poor Dad was) to the Fast Track (where Rich Dad was and where I wanted to be), but it gets easier and easier.

I've been heading for the Fast Track for most of my life. By the time Mike and I were sixteen years old, we began to separate from the crowd at school. We worked for Mike's dad in the afternoons and on the weekends. We often spent hours after work at a table with Rich Dad while he held meetings with his bankers, attorneys, accountants, brokers, investors, managers, and employees.

Mike and I learned more sitting at those meetings than we did in all our years of school—college included.

We were learning with new rules and a new way to measure success. We weren't getting A, B, or C grades, but we knew how to measure our progress.

"Report cards are what you get in school," Rich Dad told us. "When you are out of school your banker will not ask you for your report card. He will ask you for your financial statement."

✎ Field Trips

Another great learning opportunity is the field trip. No, it's not like the field trips to the natural history museum that kids take in elementary school. But one thing that's the same is that these field trips are meant to get you *out* of school and give you a new perspective. These are field trips that give you the chance to see some things in action that you may have only read about. These field trips are not so much physical excursions as they are fact-finding missions that allow you to "play along" in real-life situations. Here are some examples:

✔ Ask your parents if you can sit with them while they pay their bills.
✔ Ask your parents if you can look at their financial statement—or create one with them.
✔ Arrange to go to work with one of your parents or a friend's parent to get an idea of what a workday is like.

✔ Create a grocery budget and menu plan for your family for one week and do the grocery shopping for that week.

✔ If your parents are going to buy a car or major household appliance like a refrigerator or washing machine, go with them. Ask them to explain their decision to either pay cash or to finance the purchase in another way, and how it affects their monthly budget and financial statement.

✔ Ask your parents if they can take you to a stockbrokerage firm. It'll be best if they can prearrange the visit with a broker who is willing to talk to you about the different types of investments and their return rates, as well as the differences among corporate stocks and how mutual funds operate. Your parents may even allow you to open an account.

✔ The next time you go to McDonald's, look carefully around and think about all of the different financial players in that business and how they make their income, such as: the owner of the land and/or the building, the owner of the business, the owner of factories that contribute the various goods you see all around you, the clerks behind the counter, the hired servicepeople who keep the building running. Which of these people have assets? Which of these people spend the most time at the restaurant? How about the least amount of time?

✔ The next time you're in an apartment building, do a little math. Look at the mailboxes and count how many apartments you think are in the building. Then, estimate how much the average tenant pays per month to live there. Multiply the two numbers to see roughly what kind of monthly income the owner is getting. Then, look around and think about the expenses the owner might have in addition to the monthly mortgage payment for the building, such as maintenance or security people. This number would be subtracted from the monthly income. What kind of profit do you think the owner is making? Is it a good one? If you know someone in the building, ask if the owner is seen on the property much. How do you think the owner spends his or her time?

All of these "field trips" will allow you to understand more about (and possibly participate in) the financial matters of your family and will help you become more financially responsible.

Part 3

Creating
Your
Own
Cash Flow

Chapter 8

Moneymaking Opportunities for Teens

So, at this point you might be saying, "Okay, I understand about assets, liabilities and cash flow, but I'm just a teenager without a trust fund. How do I get some cash flowing in?"

Work to Learn, Not to Earn

There are many ways to make money, even if you're sixteen or younger. I guarantee that you—yes, *you*—can offer a skill or service that people want and need *and* are willing to pay for. If being a waiter or clerk doesn't sound tremendously exciting to you, I'm not surprised. I learned from Rich Dad, who told me to start a business instead.

You can always deliver newspapers, rake leaves in the fall, or shovel snow off sidewalks in the winter, just like your parents might have done when they were kids—but you can do it with a modern twist: Gather your friends together and turn it into a neighborhood business that makes money for all of you—even when you're not doing the labor. Instead of walking your neighbor's dog for a few bucks, for example, you can start a dog-walking business. Instead of being an employee, be an entrepreneur. When you're in business for yourself, you're in the driver's seat.

If you want to be a business owner someday but can't get it off the ground right away, selling is a very important skill you can learn in the meantime. The good news is that sales experience can be gained in hundreds of different settings, whether they're supermarkets, mall stores, or restaurants. The lessons you learn in one industry can often be applied to other industries. So just because you may work in a shoe store now, it doesn't mean you're only learning about shoes!

* * *

✎ What's the Right Job for You?

What would be your ideal line of work? Take a few moments right now to write down in your Rich Dad Journal a few careers that come to mind in one column. Then in another column write a list of jobs that you know teenagers in your area have access to. Can you draw lines to connect items in the two columns? For example, do you fantasize about owning a line of clothing someday? Why not start by trying to work in a clothing store so you can start to learn about the business? When thinking about where you'd like to work, think about *your* goals first.

If you couldn't make any connections between the two columns—or, after you've made as many connections as you can between the columns—make a third column. This is the column Rich Dad would tell me to focus on: opportunities that you can create for yourself. Maybe there are unusual jobs that you've never heard of a teen in your community doing, but that you imagine would be a learning opportunity that interests you. Just because you don't know anyone your age that has done it, why should that stop you from investigating it?

Of course, while it would be great if you could work at your favorite clothing or record store, not everyone is going to be that lucky. Remember, I didn't love my first job stocking shelves, but I did it because I believed I would learn something from Rich Dad. So, I'll say it again: *Work to learn, not to earn!*

Work Is an Exchange

When my parents told me they didn't have the money to send me to college, I told them I would find a way to pay for my own education. By that time, I'd already been earning my own money. But it wasn't the money I earned that was going to put me through school. It was the lessons I learned earning the money that actually did it.

At the age of nine, I learned a very important concept that taught me how to survive on my own: exchange. Rich Dad told me, "You can have anything you want as long as you're willing to exchange something of value for what you want." What this meant to me is that the more I gave, the more I got in return. By working for free when I was nine, I learned this lesson of exchange. I showed Rich Dad that I was willing to work in exchange for his teaching me about money.

In order to create a fair exchange, you must learn what each job is worth to you. You must look for opportunity, not salary. If you're working in a job that's worth only the amount of cash that ends up in your pocket after you receive your paycheck, that's not a good exchange. Working to earn means you're giving a certain amount of your time and usually getting back an amount of money that is equal to (or *less* than) what you feel your time is worth. Working to learn means that you're usually getting back something much greater than the time you're giving up—in addition to the cash! So, which sounds better to you?

✍ Rich Dad Q&A

What if I want to work, but my parents won't let me?

Suppose you want to get an after-school job, but your parents simply say "no." Ask them why. If the reason is that they fear it will take time away from your school studies, you need to consider whether or not they might be right.

On the other hand, if you truly want to work to *learn*, and you can convince your parents of that, they may think again. Most parents will support their kids' efforts to learn. Or, if you prove to them that you're committed to starting your own business (rather than working for minimum wage for an employer), a lot of resistant parents might change their tune, too. It's difficult to break through the common parental mindset that spending all of your free time working to get better grades is the best preparation for success. But, if your parents see you being innovative and entrepreneurial, they're likely to begin to understand what your motivations and talents are. Chances are they *do* want to nurture and encourage those qualities in you!

Business Brainstorming

A lot of young people don't even realize that there's work that's available to them even in their early teen years. If you're thirteen or younger, you can babysit, deliver newspapers, act or perform, or work for your parents in an office. At fourteen, you can also work in an office that doesn't belong to your parents, or a grocery store, retail store, restaurant, movie theater, baseball park, amusement park, or gas station. At sixteen, you can work just about anywhere—except in hazardous occupations such as storing or making explosives or driving a motor vehicle.

It's time to start brainstorming again. Here's a list of jobs where you can be in business for yourself just to get you going:

- ✧ Be a tutor.
- ✧ Teach people of all ages how to use the computer.
- ✧ Read to an older neighbor.
- ✧ Babysit for a younger neighbor.
- ✧ Be a magician at kids' birthday parties.
- ✧ Wash cars.
- ✧ Run errands. Deliver packages.
- ✧ Water plants or walk dogs while neighbors are away.
- ✧ Sew: Make alterations, cool clothes, or create costumes for children's parties.
- ✧ Before the holidays: Start a tree-decorating service.
- ✧ After the holidays: Offer a tree-removal service.
- ✧ Make personalized T-shirts or customize jackets.

✧ Be a personal assistant: Type letters, do research.

✧ In the summer you can work full time at a play group, day-care center, or local swimming pool.

✧ Put on plays or comedy sketches. Charge admission.

This is just a start. What other ideas can you come up with?

FYI: Things You Can't Do

It's important to note that there's some work that isn't okay to do if you're under eighteen. You can't drive a vehicle for your job, even though you might have a driver's license. You can't operate powered equipment or work on a ladder or scaffold, either. If you're under fourteen or fifteen (depending on where you live), you may not bake or cook.

Since different states have different laws, I strongly recommend that you check out the U.S. Department of Labor Web site (www.dol.gov) before starting a specific job. There you'll find a detailed listing of age-related rules for the whole country and for specific states. There is also a special page called "Kids & Youth," which provides a shortcut to links that'll be of interest to you, with tons of information about jobs, minimum wages, overtime rules, and other rights on the job. For example, there are rules for the maximum number of hours you can work in any given week.

Where to Look for Work

When you start looking for work, you can be on the lookout for an opportunity every waking moment. Suppose you're in a store one day and you have to wait in line a long time to pay for what you've bought. Find the manager and ask if the store could use another person to work the cash registers. Employers are looking for people who are inventive and who take initiative. Who knows? One day you may be running your own clothing company or boutique. Plenty of people who came to own their businesses started by learning the ropes at the bottom.

Here are some other places to look for work.

- ❖ Ask family, friends, neighbors, and parents of your friends. Ask everyone you know!
- ❖ Look on bulletin boards in your school, supermarkets near where you live, and the public library. If transportation is a problem, go to places that are walking distance from your home.
- ❖ Go to stores where you like to shop and ask if there are jobs available.
- ❖ Check out listings at your chamber of commerce. Most towns have chambers of commerce, usually right on Main Street, and many actually have teen job programs.
- ❖ Ask at your place of worship, community clubs, and youth associations.

✧ Go on fact-finding interviews.

✧ Check the Internet. Two good sites are:

- **www.afterschool.gov/tncareer.html** This site
  lists other sites that have jobs and internships for
  teens. An internship is a job that's usually short-
  term (over the summer or one semester) and that
  usually doesn't pay a salary.

- **www.youthrules.dol.gov** YouthRules! is geared
  to helping teens with their first experience as part
  of the workforce, whether it's an ongoing part-
  time job or summer work.

✧ Check listings in the newspaper.

✧ Go to employment agencies.

It's worth noting that as exciting as looking for work
opportunities can be, you should be careful, too. Don't
work alone or late at night. Discuss your job search with
your parents and keep them posted every step of the way.
And remember, stay away from jobs in which you raise
money for someone else.

A Few Things About Your Paycheck

The downside of working—even if you're working to
learn—is that you'll be exposed to paying taxes for the
first time. Fortunately, at your age, filing a tax return is
usually fairly straightforward.

You must pay federal taxes if you earn over a certain amount per year ($7,000 in the U.S.), which means you'll have to submit tax forms each year by April 15. And in most states, you must also pay state tax no matter what amount you make. If you decide to get a job, make sure you and your parents have investigated what your local regulations are about taxes first.

With each paycheck, a certain amount of money is also taken out and put away for your retirement, called Social Security, and Medicare. So remember that if you agree to work 10 hours a week for $5.00 an hour, you won't be taking home $50 in cash at week's end.

See why it's much better to work to learn, not to earn? It's very difficult to make a lot of money if you rely solely on your paycheck. But at least your paycheck *will* help get your cash flow in motion.

⛅ Ask an Expert/Find a Mentor

Rich Dad was my mentor when I was growing up. The best way to find out about working is to find your own mentor—someone who's successful in the field you want to pursue. Ask if you can come along with them on the job once or twice, or even several times. Be their intern.

Your mentor is like a one-on-one coach, someone you can turn to when you have questions. If you're going into business for yourself, your mentor will help you figure out what type of business would be best for you. He or she might even help you figure out what fees to charge and what to pay your employees per hour. More rewarding, though, is the fact that you'll have discovered your own personal role model who inspires you.

A mentor is someone who cares about you, too. He or she will check in with you on a regular basis and give you honest feedback on what you've done. It might be a relative, an older brother or sister of a friend, a teacher who helps you in a specific subject by suggesting books to read, or someone you work for who'll train you on the job simply because they see your potential for success.

No one ever said success was easy to come by alone. Having a mentor, or any other kind of help, is nothing to be ashamed of. In fact, a lot of famous people had mentors; without these role models who believed in them, many of these celebrities may not have achieved the wealth or fame that they eventually did.

During the next few days, ask older people you know if they have mentors now or if they had mentors growing up. Ask your teachers, your older siblings' friends, your aunts, uncles, or parents. Most of them will probably have a great story of someone who was a true inspiration to them at some point in their lives. Ask them how they met and established relationships with these people, and consider whether or not you can apply some of these lessons in your own life.

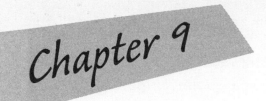

Chapter 9

Managing Your Assets

The Piggy-Bank Approach

Okay, so now you're working, looking for a job, or maybe just thinking about earning money. When you make money, you're going to need to put it somewhere. Keeping money under your mattress, as they do in cartoons and old movies, is probably not a great idea. But remember piggy banks? To a little kid, piggy banks are a great way to save because you can really watch your money grow. Nickels, dimes, and quarters have a way of piling up fast and can buy lots of bubble gum and other things that little kids buy.

You may think the old piggy bank on your dresser is just kid stuff—but you were probably a lot smarter about saving money as a little kid than you are now. What I learned from Rich Dad is that no matter what age you are, you should have a piggy bank—and not just one piggy bank. Rich Dad recommended that I have three piggy banks, each one for a specific purpose.

Piggy Bank #1 = Charity

One of the really great things about being rich is the ability to help others. Over the years I have noticed that many of the richest people in the world give money away. To be truly rich, we need to be able to give as well as to receive. Giving money away is one of the best ways to help right the wrongs of the world. It's a wonderful feeling to see a problem and know that you have the power to donate the money to a cause or group that will help make the world a better place. Buying things for yourself is great, but giving money to others is the best feeling in the world. Try it! You'll get an idea of the true power of money.

There are lots of opportunities to give. To find a charity that you feel strongly about, watch for public service announcements on television or the radio, and look through the paper for articles about foundations and charities. *The New York Times* has a column called "The Neediest Cases," that tells stories about people in need and lists the charities that will get money to them. There may be a similar column in your newspaper.

Check the Internet. Some of your favorite celebrities or authors even have their own foundations that give money away. Contributing to their charity would be a great way to feel connected to an entertainer of whom you're a big fan, or to thank a writer for the hours of enjoyable reading they've provided.

When it comes time to send money to a charity, tell your parents what you intend to do. As much as we like to think that everyone is honest, there are some scam artists out there who pretend to be raising money for charities but who are only helping themselves. Your parents can help you make sure that an organization is accredited.

When sending your contribution, it's best to send a check. If you don't have a checking account, you can pay with a money order. A check or money order is the safest way to send money through the mail and it's a good record of your contribution. Charitable contributions are tax deductible, which means that the more contributions you make, the less you pay in taxes.

Piggy Bank #2 = Savings

My second piggy bank was for savings. Rich Dad felt it was important to have enough money to cover one year's worth of expenses. Nowadays, that formula is difficult to follow, but the idea is to have a backup of savings, money that is tucked away safely for a "rainy day." This piggy bank represents security. While it's important to have something in this piggy bank, it's also not important to put *all* of your leftover income after expenses into it. Here's why:

Most saving accounts pay you interest—that is, a percentage of the total in your account—each month. It's kind of a way of encouraging you to keep your money in the bank—so the bank can use it instead. It might seem pretty exciting to have money added to your account each month as if by magic. But the truth of the matter is that the interest usually doesn't amount to much. The place where you'll see real results is putting money into your assets.

A Trip to the Bank

Go to a bank near you after school one day. (Don't forget to tell your parents where you're going. Or, invite one of your parents to go with you.)

At the bank, ask to speak with a customer-care person. They should be able to describe each type of account that they offer and explain what the current interest rates are for each. Tell them about your needs: Do you have some money that you want to put aside for a few years? Do you need to have an account that allows you to take out money when you need it? There are accounts to meet every need.

You can also take home the brochures available in the bank and read up on the different types of accounts and how you set them up. Look for the answers to these key questions: Which accounts require a minimum balance? Which accounts offer higher interest rates? Which accounts allow you to write checks and withdraw money on demand?

Piggy Bank #3 = Investments

My third piggy bank was for investments and represented risk and learning, and buying and building assets. When I was nine I used this money to invest in comic books and, later, rare coins, stocks, and real estate. As you now know, the third piggy bank is the one that Rich Dad taught me to focus on. The second piggy bank is the one that most people *think* they need to focus on. But since investments typically earn more money than savings accounts, Rich Dad knew that the third piggy bank deserved much more attention in order to create wealth.

👆 Rich Dad Q&A
Aren't piggy banks for kids?

I'll admit, the idea of three piggy banks sounds pretty childish, but it's actually very sophisticated. I still keep three piggy banks. They're a good visual reminder. Keeping your money in a piggy bank is really a metaphor for what money does if you're saving and investing wisely. Money grows!

Having money is a great opportunity to do good things in the world. Financial intelligence allows you to work or not work, to buy whatever you want without worrying about the price, or to give money away to a charity or cause that is important to you. Money without financial intelligence is money soon gone.

💡 What Would You Do if You Got $1 Million?

Years ago, there was a show on TV called "The Millionaire." Every episode began with a man showing up at someone's house with a check, and showed people's reactions to getting the money. Often people who were greedy, or who let their emotions decide how to spend the money, lost the money in a very short time. Those who better understood the power of money gave it away unselfishly, or used it well by dividing it among their own "piggy banks."

If you were a millionaire, whom in your life would you give $1 million to? How do you think they would react? How do you think they would handle the money? How would *you* spend it? What percentage would you put in each piggy bank?

Grow Your Money

You might have seen some books when you were a kid that had a picture of a boy or girl with a watering can pouring water on a "money plant." I guess this is an easy way to teach children that if they take care of their money it will grow. But what does it mean to "take care" of your money?

After learning about the three piggy banks, you might think it's all about sitting on your money. And what fun would that be? Good news: Filling those piggy banks is only a part of the formula. The other part of the formula is what may seem like exactly the opposite—it's about keeping your money *moving*. That's the best part! The fun begins once you've got some money in all of your piggy banks. . . .

Return on Investment

Rich Dad used to say, "Savers are losers." He wasn't telling us that saving money was bad. He wanted us to understand that saving had its limitations. Here's an example: Suppose I decide to buy an apartment building and rent out the apartments. I buy the building for $100,000 and use $10,000 from my savings for the down payment. I go to the bank for a mortgage, which means that I borrow the rest of the money ($90,000) from a bank to buy the building and pay that sum (plus interest) back to the bank a little at a time.

In one year, the income I get from the renters—minus what I have paid in my mortgage, taxes, and other money I pay for improvements—is able to earn back the $10,000 I originally paid in down payment. I will now take the $10,000 and buy another building, house, business, or stock. As Rich Dad would say, my money has come back very quickly. My return on my investment (R.O.I.) is 100 percent. I still own the building, but I have none of my own money in it anymore. Now all the income I receive provides infinite return on the investment. If I had kept that initial $10,000 in my savings account, the money would have gone nowhere.

Pay Yourself First

Let's go back to the three piggy banks. I had originally taken the money I needed to buy the apartment building out of piggy bank #2. As soon as I've earned some money, the first place I'm going to put my money is back into that piggy bank. This idea of paying yourself first comes from a book written by George Clason called *The Richest Man in Babylon* (Plume).

Take a look at this financial statement.

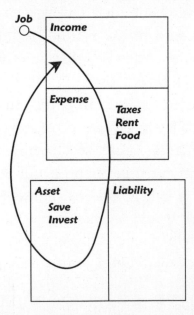

This is the financial statement of a woman who has paid herself first. Each month she puts money into the asset (income) column before she pays her monthly expenses of her mortgage and her school tuition. Even when she's a little short of money, she pays herself first. She does not dip into her savings, even when she comes up a little bit short once in a while. It makes her really think about how to make up the difference.

In the next chapter I will talk about debt. It might sound like a contradiction, but there *is* such a thing as "good" debt.

✎ Are You Rich Yet?

In the Introduction, I asked you to put an index card somewhere in the middle of the book as a milestone on your journey toward getting rich. How are you doing? Take a moment now and write down in your Rich Dad Journal your thoughts about what has changed so far. Do you feel you're spending less? Or, are you at least more aware of how you spend your money? Are you more confident that changing the way you think about money will put you on the path toward financial freedom?

Chapter 10

Managing
Your
Debt

Good Debt and Bad Debt

You're probably wondering how *managing* debt—instead of getting *rid* of debt—can be an important lesson in a book about getting rich. I used to think that rich people couldn't know the meaning of debt—and that the words "rich" and "debt" could not exist in the same sentence, or even in the same person's life.

My Poor Dad worked hard all his life to get out of debt. Rich Dad worked hard all his life to get into debt. "If you want to be rich," he would say, "you must know the difference between good debt and bad debt."

Credit Card Basics

When you get a cash gift for your birthday, what's the first thing you do? Rush out and spend it, right? It's like someone telling you not to think of the word "elephant." Hard, isn't it? I have the feeling that as soon as I told you *not* to think of that word, it would leap into your head. I know that telling someone not to spend money can trigger a similar reaction.

If you can't resist temptations to buy doodads and have trouble keeping money in your wallet, having a credit card makes it even harder to hang on to your money. With real money, you actually see the bills. At the cash register, you have to take the money out of your wallet, count it out, pay for the item, and get your change. With a credit card, all you take out is a piece of plastic that you hand to the cashier or person behind the counter (or else you just swipe it through a machine) and sign for it. That's it! The process is so easy, you hardly know you're paying for something. And that can be dangerous.

The Downward Spiral

Having a credit card can get you into trouble. Here's how it works. You get a card in the mail with a low introductory interest rate. With this magic piece of plastic, you can now buy things with money you don't have. You buy whatever you like. Having a credit card is like having a blank check—until the bill comes. It's surprising how quickly your purchases make it to your billing statement, that neat listing that gives the date and amount of each and every one of your purchases. And here's where the trouble really starts to spiral.

The credit card statement has a date of when your payment is due and the amount due. Not only does it give the full amount due but the minimum payment due. Hmm . . . ten dollars doesn't seem like much, you figure. I'll just pay the minimum until my purchases are paid for.

If you pay off your debt using the minimum payment option, chances are pretty high that whatever you bought will break or go out of style long before you pay for it. Paying the minimum amount due on your balance usually means you'll have to pay the price of an extremely high interest rate. In case you didn't know, that's the percentage of your grand total owed that is *added* to your bill each month. So each month your bill grows without your even buying anything new. It's worse than spending money on a liability—it's almost as if you were flushing the money right down the toilet.

Let's say you buy a flat-screen TV for $2,000, and you pay it off over time using the minimum payment. It could take you thirty years to pay it off if your card charges 18% interest.

Take control of your credit card bills before they spin out of control. The older you get, the harder it gets. It's good to start practicing discipline now. The next time you and your friends hang out in the mall, decide to do some window shopping, instead of splurging on doodads that'll be out of fashion in a few months. And if you do buy something on a credit card, make an effort to pay for it in full when the bill comes.

Credit cards can be your worst nightmare, but not always. In fact, if you use a credit card wisely—that is, if you pay your bill on time—you'll have an excellent opportunity to establish a good credit rating. That will help you later in life when you need to borrow money to buy assets that will bring you passive income—such as buying real estate, an income-producing asset. Credit cards also help you keep track of how you are spending your money.

One Dollar at a Time

Often when I give speeches, I tell people that with each dollar bill that comes their way, they have the power to determine their destiny. You can too. Will you be rich or poor in your life? Spend that dollar foolishly and you've chosen to be poor. Spend it on liabilities time after time, and you'll always be middle class. Learn how to get assets and you'll be choosing wealth as your goal and your future. The choice is yours—every day with every dollar you receive and every dollar you spend. This is an awesome responsibility and it's an amazing feeling of power. Your financial future is in your own hands!

Your Financial Head Start

In 1990, my best friend Mike took over his father's empire, and is, in fact, doing an even better job than his dad did. He's now grooming his own son to take his place, just the way his dad had groomed us. Because he persisted in working to *learn* (not to earn) starting at the age of nine, Mike gained financial intelligence. He's the kind of person who has created his own luck and he created his own money. He took what life handed him and made it better.

I retired in 1994—when I was at the age of 47, and my wife, Kim, was 37. Retirement doesn't mean not working. We can work or not work as we choose, and our wealth grows automatically. Our assets grow by themselves. It's like we have planted a money tree. We watered it and took care of it for years and then it didn't need us anymore. Its roots have gone down deep enough. Now the tree is providing shade for our enjoyment.

When I was young I did not always understand what Rich Dad was saying to me. As with most great teachers, his words continued to teach me for years. His words and lessons are still with me today.

Choose Wisely!

I have only one last bit of advice for you right now: Choose your friends and mentors wisely. Be careful from whom you take advice. If you want to go somewhere, it's best to find someone who's already been there.

For example, if you decide you're going to climb Mount Everest next year, obviously you'd seek advice from someone who had climbed the mountain before. However, when it comes to climbing financial mountains, most people ask advice from people who are stuck in financial swamps.

Rich Dad encouraged me always to have a coach or mentor. He constantly said, "Professionals have coaches. Amateurs do not."

For example, I play golf and I take lessons, but I don't have a full-time coach. This is probably why I pay money to play golf instead of getting paid to play. Yet, when it comes to the games of business and investing, I do have coaches—several of them. Why do I have coaches? I have coaches because I get paid to play those games.

So choose your mentors wisely. It's one of the most important things you can do. One of the other most important things you can do is choose your *friends* wisely.

✎ The People You Spend Your Time with Are Your Future

Get out your Rich Dad Journal and write down the six people you spend the most time with. Remember that the qualifier is whom you spend the most time with, not the type of your relationship. (Do not read any further until you have written down your six names.)

I was at a seminar about fifteen years ago when the instructor asked us to do the same. I wrote down my six names. He asked us to look at the names we had written, and he announced, "You are looking at your future. The six people you spend the most time with are your future."

The six people you spend the most time with may not necessarily always be personal friends. For some of you it may be your teachers, family, or members of your church. My list was pretty revealing once I began to look below the surface. I gained insights about myself that I liked and even more that I didn't like.

The instructor had us go around the room and meet with other people to discuss our lists. The more I discussed my list with other people, and the more I listened to them, the more I realized I needed to make some changes.

In reality, this exercise has little to do with the people you're spending your time with. It has everything to do with where you're going and what you're doing with your life.

Fifteen years after I did this exercise, the people I spend the most time with are all different except one. The five others from my earlier list are still dear friends, but we rarely see each other. They're great people and they're happy with their lives. My change had only to do with me. I wanted to change my future. To successfully change my future, I had to change my thoughts and, as a result, the people I spent time with. Choose to spend time with people who understand and appreciate your vision and goals. Even better, choose people who share them!

What I Got from My Two Dads

Both of my dads were generous men. Both made it a practice to give first. Teaching was one of their ways of giving. The more they gave, the more they received. In a way, I became both dads as I grew up. One part of me is a capitalist who loves the game of money and making it. This other side of me is a socially responsible teacher who is deeply concerned with the ever-widening gap between the haves and the have-nots.

A Strong Foundation

Mike and I were both given a strong foundation for our knowledge. We learned that our strongest asset is our minds. If it's trained to see opportunity, it can create great wealth in a short amount of time. Mike and I learned this lesson when we were kids. Now that we're adults, we're still building on our strong foundation. What Rich Dad taught me still applies. That's what I hope this book has done for you. I hope that I've been as good a teacher to you as Rich Dad was for me.

I hope that with greater financial literacy, you'll be able to choose exactly what you want to do with your life, whether it's knowing how to run a major record label, owning real estate, becoming a forest ranger, or building businesses. With knowledge of how to take care of yourself financially, you'll also be able to take care of others, whether it's giving money to charity or being able to give friends and family members the things they want and need without worry. This will help you lead a fuller, richer life.

Thank you for reading this book.
Robert Kiyosaki

A Note From
Sharon Lechter

Super You

You can do anything you want. Now that you have the basic tools of your financial education, you have real choices about your financial future. I have one question for you: What will you do with your financial head start? I want to know. I want you to write and tell me what your dreams are.

Robert and I offer you a challenge. We would like to ask you to stretch and grow and find opportunities to create wealth in interesting and innovative ways—and I invite you to tell me about it. Through this book, we've begun a journey together. You've read the book, you've visited the Web site, and I hope you've played the games. I would like to know what direction your journey is taking now.

Thank you, and I look forward to hearing from you.

Sharon Lechter

Please write to us at teens@richdad.com

Glossary

Asset: Something that puts money "in your pocket" on a regular basis, with the least amount of direct work.

Balance Sheet: A snapshot of your assets and liabilities that gives you an overview of your financial status.

Business: A system of the purchase and sale of goods and/or services with the intent to make a profit.

Capital: Cash or something of an agreed-upon value. Money or property owned or employed in a business.

Cash Flow: Cash coming in (as income) and cash going out (as expenses). The direction of the cash flow determines whether something is defined as income, an expense, an asset, or a liability.

Down Payment: A percentage of the purchase price an investor pays for an investment. The remainder of the price is then financed through other means.

Income Statement: A form showing your income and expenses over a period of time. Also called a profit and loss statement.

Liability: Something that takes money "out of your pocket."

Mortgage: If you're financing your real estate, the property is used as collateral against the amount of money you're borrowing. The mortgage is the security instrument.

Mutual Fund: A variety of stocks, bonds, or securities grouped together, managed by a professional investment company and purchased by individual investors through shares. The shares possess no direct ownership value in the various companies.

Passive Income: Income generated from your investments, such as interest, dividends, and real-estate rentals, with a minimum amount of work.

R.O.I.: Return on Investment. Rich Dad views R.O.I. as cash on cash return, or the percentage of return on capital (goods in your possession that work toward bringing in income) from an investment. Example: An apartment building costs $500,000. You pay $100,000 as a down payment. It generates a monthly cash flow of $2,000. Your R.O.I., or cash on cash return, is $2,000 x 12 ($24,000) divided by $100,000, or 24 percent.

Robert T. Kiyosaki

Robert Kiyosaki is an investor, entrepreneur, educator, and author.

Born and raised in Hawaii, Robert Kiyosaki is a fourth-generation Japanese-American. After graduating from college in New York, Robert joined the Marine Corps and served in Vietnam as an officer and helicopter gunship pilot. Following the war, Robert worked for the Xerox Corporation in sales. In 1977, he started a company that brought the first nylon and Velcro "surfer wallets" to market. And in 1985 he founded an international education company that taught business and investing to tens of thousands of students throughout the world.

In 1994 Robert sold his business and, through his investments, was able to retire at the age of 47.

During his short-lived retirement, Robert wrote the bestselling book *Rich Dad Poor Dad*, which to date has sold over 17 million copies worldwide. The success of *Rich Dad Poor Dad* paved the way for the Rich Dad series of books—currently nine books in total. Most all of these books have earned spots on the bestseller lists of *The New York Times*, *The Wall Street Journal*, *BusinessWeek*, *USA Today*, and others.

Prior to becoming a bestselling author, Robert created the educational board game CASHFLOW® 101—to teach individuals the financial and investment strategies that his rich dad spent years teaching him. It was those same strategies that allowed Robert to retire at age 47. Hundreds of "CASH-FLOW® Clubs," independent of The Rich Dad® Company, have sprung up throughout the world. Thousands of people get together on a regular basis and play CASHFLOW® 101.

With the launch of the electronic version of CASHFLOW® 101, members of the Rich Dad community around the world can unite in playing and learning together—online. CASHFLOW® 202, the advanced game, is now gaining great popularity in both the board game and electronic versions.

In Robert's words, "We go to school to learn to work hard for money. I write books and create products that *teach people how to have money work hard for them*. Then they can enjoy the luxuries of this great world we live in."

The Rich Dad Company is the collaborative effort of Robert Kiyosaki, Kim Kiyosaki, and Sharon Lechter, who, in 1997, set out to elevate the financial literacy of people throughout the world.

Sharon Lechter

 C.P.A., co-author of the Rich Dad book series, CEO and cofounder of Rich Dad's Organization, has dedicated her professional efforts to the field of education. She graduated with honors from Florida State University with a degree in accounting and started her career with Coopers & Lybrand. Sharon has held various management positions with computer, insurance, and publishing companies while maintaining her professional credentials as a C.P.A.

Sharon and husband, Michael Lechter, have been married for over 20 years and are parents to three children, Phillip, Shelly, and William. As her children grew, she became actively involved in their education and served in leadership positions in their schools. She became a vocal activist in the areas of mathematics, computers, reading, and writing education.

In 1989 she joined forces with the inventor of the first electronic "talking book" and helped him expand the electronic book industry to a multimillion-dollar international market.

Today she remains a pioneer in developing new technologies to bring education into children's lives in ways that are innovative, challenging, and fun. As co-author of the Rich Dad books and CEO of that company, she focuses her efforts in the arena of financial education.

"Our current educational system has not been able to keep pace with the global and technological changes in the world today," Sharon states. "We must teach our young people the skills—both scholastic and financial—that they need to not only survive but to flourish in the world."

A committed philanthropist, Sharon "gives back" to the world communities as both a volunteer and a benefactor. She directs the Foundation for Financial Literacy and is a strong advocate of education and the need for improved financial literacy.

Sharon and Michael were honored by Childhelp USA, a national organization founded to eradicate child abuse in the United States, as recipients of the 2002 "Spirit of the Children" Award. And, in May of 2002, Sharon was named Chairman of the Board for the Phoenix chapter of Childhelp USA.

As an active member of Women's Presidents Organization, she enjoys networking with other professional women across the country.

Robert Kiyosaki, her business partner and friend, says "Sharon is one of the few natural entrepreneurs I have ever met. My respect for her continues to grow every day that we work together."

Time Warner Book Group Chairman, Larry Kirshbaum, has stated: "What Sharon and Robert have accomplished with Rich Dad is a feat that is unprecedented in the publishing arena."

The Rich Dad Company is the collaborative effort of Robert Kiyosaki, Kim Kiyosaki, and Sharon Lechter, who, in 1997, set out to elevate the financial literacy of people throughout the world.

The Foundation for Financial Literacy

With the success of the Rich Dad books and products, Robert and Kim Kiyosaki and Sharon Lechter have created the Foundation for Financial Literacy. This foundation was created to support educational, charitable, religious, and scientific programs and organizations that utilize financial education to teach the difference between earned, passive, and portfolio income and educate individuals to convert earned income into passive and portfolio income. The Foundation's mission reflects that of the Rich Dad Organization: to elevate the financial well-being of humanity.

The Foundation for Financial Literacy, a 501 (c)(3) nonprofit organization established in 1999, has funded numerous grant applications through individual and corporate donations. See www.ffliteracy.org for more information.

Keep reading to find out more information
about some of the Rich Dad books,
games, and other products.

Robert Kiyosaki's Edumercial:
An Educational Commercial

The Three Incomes

In the world of accounting, there are three different types of income: earned, passive, and portfolio. When my real dad said to me, "Go to school, get good grades and find a safe, secure job," he was recommending I work for earned income. When my rich dad said, "The rich don't work for money; they have their money work for them," he was talking about passive income and portfolio income. Passive income, in most cases, is derived from real estate investments. Portfolio income is income derived from paper assets, such as stocks, bonds, and mutual funds.

Rich Dad used to say, "The key to becoming wealthy is the ability to convert earned income into passive income and/or portfolio income as quickly as possible." He would say, "The taxes are highest on earned income. The least taxed income is passive income. That is another reason why you want your money working hard for you. The government taxes the income you work hard for more than the income your money works hard for."

The Key to Financial Freedom

The key to financial freedom and great wealth is a person's ability or skill to convert earned income into passive income and/or portfolio income. That is the skill that my rich dad spent a lot of time teaching Mike and me. Having that skill is the reason my wife Kim and I are financially free, never needing to work again. We continue to work because we choose to. Today we own a real estate investment company for passive income and participate in private placements and initial public offerings of stock for portfolio income.

Investing to become rich requires a different set of personal skills—skills essential for financial success as well as low-risk and high-investment returns. In other words, knowing how to create assets that buy other assets. The problem is that gaining the basic education and experience required is often time consuming, frightening, and expensive, especially when you make mistakes with your own money. That is why I created the patented educational board games trademarked as CASHFLOW®.

Rich Dad Poor Dad

What the rich teach their kids about money that the poor and middle class do not! Learn how to have your money work for you and why you don't need to earn a high income to be rich.

The book that "rocked" the financial world.

J.P. Morgan declares *Rich Dad Poor Dad* "a must-read for millionaires."
—*The Wall Street Journal*

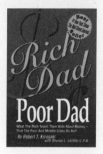

"A starting point for anyone looking to gain control of their financial future."
—*USA Today*

Rich Dad's Rich Kid Smart Kid

Give your child a financial head start. Awaken your child's love of learning how to be financially free. Imagine the results you'll see when they start early!

This book is written for parents who value education, want to give their child a financial and academic head start in life, and are willing to take an active role to make it happen. *Rich Kid Smart Kid* is designed to help you give your child the same inspiring and practical financial knowledge that Robert's rich dad gave him. Learn how to awaken your child's love of learning.

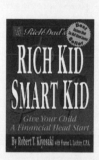

Rich Dad's Success Stories

Learn why you're never too young to achieve financial success and read the many stories from people of all ages. Each story is inspiring because instead of people now feeling entitled to have money handed to them, they are setting goals, achieving them, and creating income—they are learning to take control of their lives. This book is about real-life people who followed the Rich Dad lessons to take control of their financial lives.

CASHFLOW® 101

CASHFLOW® 101 is an educational program that teaches accounting, finance, and investing at the same time and makes learning fun.

Learn how to get out of the rat race and onto the fast track where your money works for you instead of you working hard for your money. The educational program, CASHFLOW® 101, includes three audiocassettes, which reveal distinctions on CASHFLOW® 101 as well as valuable investment information and a video titled *The Secrets of the Rich*.

CASHFLOW® 101 is recommended for adults and children ages 10 and older.

CASHFLOW® 202

CASHFLOW® 202 teaches you the advanced business and investing techniques used by technical investors by adding volatility to the game. It teaches the advanced investment techniques of "shortselling stock," "put-options," "call-options," "straddles," and real estate exchanges.

You must have CASHFLOW® 101 in order to play CASHFLOW® 202. This package contains new game sheets, new playing cards, and 4 audiocassettes.

CASHFLOW® for KIDS

Give your children the financial head start necessary to thrive in today's fast-paced and changing world. Schools teach children how to work for money. CASHFLOW® for KIDS teaches children how to have money work for them.

CASHFLOW® for KIDS is a complete educational package, which includes the book and audiocassette titled Rich Dad's Guide to Raising Your Child's Financial IQ.

CASHFLOW® for KIDS is recommended for children ages 6 older.

"Move over, Monopoly®... A new board game that aims to teach people how to get rich is gaining fans the world over!"

—*The New York Times*, February 1, 2004

MONOPOLY® is a trademark of Hasbro, Inc.

CASHFLOW® THE E-GAME

What's your dream? Freedom of time? Unlimited resources to travel the world? Whatever it may be, CASHFLOW® THE E-GAME teaches you how to get out of the Rat Race and onto the FastTrack. Learn about money and finances in a fun, interactive environment to make more informed choices about money in your everyday life!

Play and compete with others across the world in the online community through the multiplayer feature. Discover how to become rich and financially free on a small or large salary!

CASHFLOW® for KIDS at Home

Discover CASHFLOW® for KIDS, a fun game created to teach your child the subjects of money and investing. A family's attitude about money is a powerful influence on a child from a very early age. The more your children play, the higher their financial IQ will become.

Learn the difference between an asset and a liability! Discover the three types of income—Earned (where you work for money), Passive, and Portfolio (where your money works for you!). Inspire an interest in the subject of money with your child!

CASHFLOW® 202 THE E-GAME

In the real world of investing there are WINNERS and LOSERS. Losers are always hoping the markets will keep going up—winners don't care! In this interactive hands-on game you will discover what few people ever learn— how to profit in up and down markets. You'll learn the tools of a technical investor; short selling, call & put options, real estate options—key tools of winning investors. With CASHFLOW® 202 THE E-GAME you can challenge other 202 gamers worldwide via the Internet with the online multiplayer feature. You will then be spending time with people just like you . . . people whose destiny it is to be Masters of their own Financial Universe.

Please Help Make a Difference

Money is a life skill—but we don't teach our children about money in school. I am asking for your help in getting financial education into the hands of interested teachers and school administrators.

RichKidSmartKid.com was created as an innovative and interactive Web site designed to convey key concepts about money and finance in ways that are fun and challenging . . . and educational for young people in grades K through 12. It contains 4 mini-games that teach:

> Assets vs. Liabilities
> Good Debt vs. Bad Debt
> Importance of Charity
> Passive Income vs. Earned Income

AND, schools may also register at www.richkidsmartkid.com to receive a FREE download of our electronic version of CASHFLOW® for KIDS at School.

How You Can Make a Difference

Play CASHFLOW® for KIDS and CASHFLOW® 101 with family and friends and share the richkidsmartkid.com Web site with your local teachers and school administrators.

Join me now in taking financial education to our schools and e-mail me of your interest at Iwill@richdad.com. Together we can better prepare our children for the financial world they will face.

Thank you!

Sharon L. Lechter